First World War
and Army of Occupation
War Diary
France, Belgium and Germany

39 DIVISION
Headquarters, Branches and Services
Royal Army Veterinary Corps
Assistant Director Veterinary Services
5 March 1916 - 31 January 1919

WO95/2573/3

The Naval & Military Press Ltd
www.nmarchive.com
Published in association with The National Archives

Published by

The Naval & Military Press Ltd

Unit 10 Ridgewood Industrial Park,

Uckfield, East Sussex,

TN22 5QE England

Tel: +44 (0) 1825 749494

www.naval-military-press.com

www.nmarchive.com

This diary has been reprinted in facsimile from the original. Any imperfections are inevitably reproduced and the quality may fall short of modern type and cartographic standards.

© Crown Copyright
Images reproduced by permission of The National Archives, London, England, 2015.

Contents

Document type	Place/Title	Date From	Date To
Heading	WO95/2573/3		
Heading	39th Division A.D. Vety Services Mar 1916-Jan 1919		
Heading	War Diary A.D.V.S. 39th Division From March 1st. 1916 To March 31st. 1916 Volume No. 1		
War Diary	Harve	05/03/1916	07/03/1916
War Diary	Blaringhem	08/03/1916	28/03/1916
War Diary	Lestrem.	29/03/1916	31/03/1916
Heading	War. Diary A.D.V.S. 39th Division From April 1st 1916. To April 30th 1916 Volume. No. 2		
War Diary	Lestrum	01/04/1916	17/04/1916
War Diary	Locon	18/04/1916	30/06/1916
Heading	War Diary-July 1916 A.D.V.S. Vol 5		
War Diary	Locon	01/07/1916	08/07/1916
War Diary	Bethune	09/07/1916	14/07/1916
War Diary	Locon.	15/07/1916	31/07/1916
War Diary	Locon	01/07/1916	07/07/1916
War Diary	Bethune	08/07/1916	14/07/1916
War Diary	Locon	15/07/1916	31/07/1916
War Diary	Locon	16/07/1916	12/08/1916
War Diary	Roellecourt	13/08/1916	24/08/1916
War Diary	Bus.	25/08/1916	27/08/1916
War Diary	Acheux.	28/08/1916	02/10/1916
War Diary	Hedauville.	03/10/1916	07/10/1916
War Diary	Bouzincourt	08/10/1916	16/11/1916
War Diary	Doullens	17/11/1916	17/11/1916
War Diary	Hazebrouck	18/11/1916	18/11/1916
War Diary	Esquelbecq.	19/11/1916	14/12/1916
War Diary	St Sixthe	15/12/1916	15/01/1917
War Diary	Poperinghe	16/01/1917	28/02/1917
War Diary	Renninghelst	01/03/1917	30/04/1917
War Diary	Border Camp	01/05/1917	03/07/1917
War Diary	Query Camp.	04/07/1917	07/08/1917
War Diary	Meteren	08/08/1917	31/08/1917
War Diary	Westoutre	01/09/1917	12/09/1917
War Diary	De Zon Camp	13/09/1917	23/09/1917
War Diary	Zevecoten	24/09/1917	28/09/1917
War Diary	St Jans Cappel	29/09/1917	16/10/1917
War Diary	De Zon Camp.	17/10/1917	16/11/1917
War Diary	Westoutre	17/11/1917	30/11/1917
War Diary	Steenvoorde	01/12/1917	10/12/1917
War Diary	Nielles Lez Blecquin.	11/12/1917	30/12/1917
War Diary	Border Camp.	31/12/1917	22/01/1918
War Diary	Proven	23/01/1918	24/01/1918
War Diary	Mericourt Sur Somme	25/01/1918	02/02/1918
War Diary	Nurlu.	03/02/1918	12/03/1918
War Diary	Haut Allaines.	13/03/1918	03/04/1918
War Diary	Andainville	04/04/1918	10/04/1918
War Diary	Eperlecques.	11/04/1918	06/06/1918
War Diary	Nielles Lez Ardres.	07/06/1918	15/08/1918
War Diary	Varengeville Sur Mer.	16/08/1918	31/01/1919

W095/25733

39TH DIVISION

A. D. VETY SERVICES

MAR 1916 - JAN 1919

ADVS
39D
Vol. 1

<u>Confidential</u>

<u>War Diary</u>

<u>A.D.V.S. 39th Division</u>

From March 1st 1916 — To March 31st 1916

Volume No. 1

W.G. Barnes Major AVC

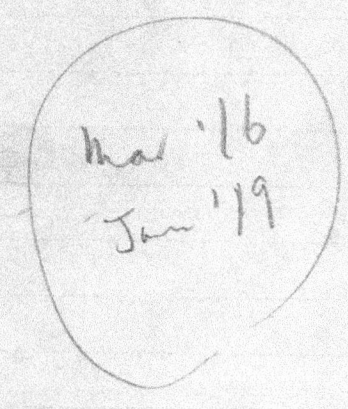
Mar '16
Jan '19

Army Form C. 2118

WAR DIARY
or
INTELLIGENCE SUMMARY
(Erase heading not required.)

Instructions regarding War Diaries and Intelligence Summaries are contained in F.S. Regs., Part II. and the Staff Manual respectively. Title Pages will be prepared in manuscript.

Place	Date	Hour	Summary of Events and Information	Remarks and references to Appendices
Havre	5.3.16		Arrived on Sunday morning. Visited Kitty Hospital re horses transferred.	W/s/Barns
"	6.3.16		Left Havre & proceeded to Abbeville by motor. Breakdown had to proceed to Rouen for repairs.	W/s/Barns
	7.3.16		Left Abbeville for Bèaringhem	
Bèaringhem	8.3.16		Visited 174 Bde & 179 R.F.A. re enquiry horses found the standing very bad. Horses up to knees in mud. Routine office work	W/s/Barns
	9.3.16		Visited Police horse & had a walk from D.D.V.S. 1st Army. Motors to arrival units and horses left by 4 out going divisions. Visited position of M.V.S. Usual Routine office work	W/s/Barns
	10.3.16		Inspected H.Q. Train horses and 186 Bde R.F.A. was informed that motor cars would be Killed & that I had no motor claim, required car. It was conducted to home. Visited Thirnes Station re arrival of 50th M.V.S. attached to 39th Division. M.V.S. arrived gave orders to the O.C. as to location of H.Q.	W/s/Barns
	11.3.16		Visited M.V.S. and 116th Bde, & 179th R.F.A. & R. G.R.F.A Routine office work	W/s/Barns
	12.3.16		Visited Unattached 9th Division & 34th Div. interviewed a D.V.S. 34th Division. visited D.D.V.S. 1st Army by request at 6 P.M. Routine office work.	W/s/Barns
	13.3.16		Visited D.A.C. met a D.V.S. & 9th Div. and arranged re supervision of the D.A.C. Visited 133 & 134 Fld. Amb. Inspected horses & Routine office work	W/s/Barns

Army Form C. 2118

WAR DIARY
or
INTELLIGENCE SUMMARY
(Erase heading not required.)

Instructions regarding War Diaries and Intelligence Summaries are contained in F. S. Regs., Part II. and the Staff Manual respectively. Title Pages will be prepared in manuscript.

Place	Date	Hour	Summary of Events and Information	Remarks and references to Appendices
Beauquesne	14.3.16		Visited 184th R.F.A. at Beauquesne & 118th Inf. Bde. inspected horses. Routine office work	W&D
	15.3.16		Visited 5 Coy M.V.S. inspected horses prior to evacuation. Visited eyesight H.9. 118th H.Q. & Routine office work	W&D
	16.3.16		Visited 149th & 186th R.F.A. Divl. Amm. Col. at daily. Motored with A.D.M.S. & Routine office work (Horses evacuated by 5th M.V.S.)	W&D
	17.3.16		Visited 119th Inf. Bde. & 184th & 174th Bde R.F.A. Motored with D.A.D.O.S. conference with Divl. Vety. Officers at daily & Routine office work	W&D
	18.3.16		Visited Sig. Coy. (Divl) R.E. & 204 coy A.S.C. & 118th H.Q. & Routine office work	W&D
	19.3.16		Visited D.D.V.S. 1st Army Area. & 184th R.F.A. routine office work	W&D
	20.3.16		Motored to daily & Talmas visited 186th & 174th Bde R.F.A. Routine office work	W&D
	21.3.16		Visited 118 th Bde. each 2 horses. Visited H.Q. 118th in coy with V.O. in charge	W&D
	22.3.16		Visited eyesight Corps. & Routine office work Visited M.V.S. and inspected horses for evacuation. & Routine office work	W&D
	23.3.16		Motored with A.D.M.S. to daily & Talmas visited Divl Train A.D.C. and inspected horses. Evacuated (24 Horses & 2 Mules) from M.V.S. & Routine office work	W&D

Army Form C. 2118

WAR DIARY
or
INTELLIGENCE SUMMARY
(Erase heading not required.)

Instructions regarding War Diaries and Intelligence Summaries are contained in F.S. Regs., Part II. and the Staff Manual respectively. Title Pages will be prepared in manuscript.

Place	Date	Hour	Summary of Events and Information	Remarks and references to Appendices
Blaringhem	24.3.16		Inspected R.E. horses had conference with Div Vety officers. Routine office work	W43
"	25.3.16		Visited 118th Bde. D.A.C. & 133 & 134 Field Ambulances Routine office work	W43
	26.3.16		Routine office work no cars obtainable	
	27.3.16		Visited daily 8/174th Bde. R.F.A. emptied horses found abandoned had about 18th Bde. R.F.A. Routine office work evacuation of 2 sick horses & 4 mules By 50th M.S. Ary B	W43
	28.3.16		Moved from Blaringhem to Lestrem. Left 2 horses unable to travel one belonging to G.O.C. and other to R.E. Routine office work.	W43
Lestrem	29.3.16		Inspected Horses 116th Bde. & visited 50th M.V.S. 133 Fld Amb. Routine office work	W43
	30.3.16		Visited St G arranged time for casting of 2 horses. Visited Vey. by lines. Routine office work.	W43
	31.3.16		Motored to St. Venant & inspected Divisional Artillery had to remain at St Venant for car to return to Lestrem. Routine office work	W43

ADVS 39D
Vol 2

Confidential
War Diary
A.D.V.S 39th Division
From April 1st 1916.   To April 30th 1916
Volume - No. 2

W G Barnes Major AVC

WAR DIARY
or
INTELLIGENCE SUMMARY

Army Form C. 2118

Place	Date	Hour	Summary of Events and Information	Remarks and references to Appendices
Lisburn	1.4.16		Visited 116th Bde. Lines & inspected horses retired mares in foal to be sent to M.V.S. also horses sometimes hung scattered. It took all day. Returned to made weekly returns of ordinary routine work	W.E. Barnes
"	2.4.16		Visited L.M.V.S. at Lisburn. Inspected Place horses & M.G. horses. Visited 287th Coy R.S.C. at north of Lisburn. Routine office work	W.E. Barnes
	3.4.16		Visited Artillery Brigades of D.A.C at Bourey & 174th Bde R.F.A sent mares in foal to M.V.S. Routine office work	W.E. Barnes
	4.4.16		Visited Divisional Cavalry D.A.C & Generals horses at Blarington. Place horses and D.H.Q. brackets of 13 horses & 2 mules. Routine office work.	W.E. Barnes
	5.4.16		Visited 119th Inf. Brigade at La Gorgue & Merville & visited South Irish horse & had case of suspected colic, cyclist transport sent one horse aged and weak. No M.V.S. General office work	W.E. Barnes
	6.4.16		Visited 116th Inf. Bde & 225th R.E. Visited M.V.S. Office work	W.E. Barnes
	7.4.16		Visited all Brigades of Artillery. use of car Refused sent it back at 1.30 A.m. and had to wait at St. Vennant to meet Vety. Officers had conference and received weekly returns sent for by the D.A.D.S car	W.E. Barnes

Army Form C. 2118

WAR DIARY
or
INTELLIGENCE SUMMARY
(Erase heading not required.)

Instructions regarding War Diaries and Intelligence Summaries are contained in F. S. Regs., Part II. and the Staff Manual respectively. Title Pages will be prepared in manuscript.

Place	Date	Hour	Summary of Events and Information	Remarks and references to Appendices
Lozinghem	8.4.16		Visited 11/7th Inf. Bde & 13 Gloucesters. Met V.O. of 33rd Div. who visited those units being temporary attached to 33rd Div. Visited Hd. Q. Coy A.S.C Div. Cavalry. Returned by D.A.D.V.S. Car. evacuated 22 horses & prepared returns.	Col. Barnes
"	9.4.16		Visited in company with Interpreter a horse belonging to a farmer at Pernes said to be wounded by trench mortar. Assessed damage.	Col. Barnes
	10.4.16		Visited Hd. Q. horses & Sig. Coy. horses. Visited all Div. Artillery Brigades at request of D.A.Q.M.G. as to casualties in horses. Requisition for Remounts instructed V.O. No hay attention to shoeing and stable management. Routine office work.	Col. Barnes
	11.4.16		Visited M.V.S. re complaint of coush by R.C.O. on a civilian horse. Hd. Q. horses & Routine office work.	Col. Barnes
	12.4.16		Visited Hd. Q. horses. Received circular relating to outbreak of a disease at Romey. Also were to visit 16th Bosse & Derby. Routine office work.	Col. Barnes
	13.4.16		Proceeded to Lozon in connection with move of Divison. Inspected horses of M.V.S returned and inspected horses of Hd. Q. Visited 118th 2/L Inf. Bde in company with V.O. in charge. Evacuation of horses by M.V.S. Notified D.D.V.S. 1st Army forwarded Return of same to D.A.Q.M.G. (Evacuated 14 horses 2 mules)	Col. Barnes

Army Form C. 2118

WAR DIARY
or
INTELLIGENCE SUMMARY
(Erase heading not required.)

Instructions regarding War Diaries and Intelligence Summaries are contained in F. S. Regs., Part II. and the Staff Manual respectively. Title Pages will be prepared in manuscript.

Place	Date	Hour	Summary of Events and Information	Remarks and references to Appendices
Lahore	14.4.16		Visited Lt. Tennant and met V.O. who returned unwashed horses 184, 186 & 194 B.S. R.F.A also South Irish Horse & 284th Bgy. A.O.C. Routine office work	Col. Barnes
	15.4.16		Routine office work. Visited 116th Inf. Bde. & M.V.S. evacuated (16 horses) Notified C.C. Re cast of the D.D.V.S. 1st Army. also V.O. Illinois	Col. Barnes
	16.4.16		Visited M.V.S. and assisted in demonstrating to V.O. Intra-dermal Palpebral test. Attended Vety. conference at Aire in afternoon.	Col. Barnes
	17.4.16		Motored with A.D.V.S. 35th Div. to A.D.V.S. 19th Div. Moved H.Q. Dir-H.Q. Routine office work	Col. Barnes
Lozon	18.4.16		Visited B.A.C. 119th R.F.A. and inspected horses and Visited M.V.S. and 116th Bde. received notification Re horse evacuated by 119th Bde. Amm. Col. through 50th M.V. Proceeding to Mallow Vet. at No. 13 Vety. Hospital and proceeded to inspect should not also to hospital. Clandro. Routine office work. Notified V.O. Re horse from 119th R.F.O. reached & gave instructions re testing of all horses in the Division. Routine office work superintended testing of horses in 119th B.A.C.	Col. Barnes
	19.4.16		Visited 119th H.Q. also B.A.C. 184th R.F.A.	Col. Barnes
	20.4.16		Visited B.A.C. 119th R.F.A. and inspected reactors horses noted. Found 4 confirmed & 6 doubtful reactors. Noted on the eye. Routine office work. Notified D.D.V.S. 1st Army. Re same.	Col. Barnes

Army Form C. 2118

WAR DIARY
or
INTELLIGENCE SUMMARY
(Erase heading not required.)

Instructions regarding War Diaries and Intelligence Summaries are contained in F. S. Regs., Part II. and the Staff Manual respectively. Title Pages will be prepared in manuscript.

Place	Date	Hour	Summary of Events and Information	Remarks and references to Appendices
Locon	21.4.16		Visited 199th B.A.C. & tried Reason's method of destroying cases. English method. Routine office work. Visited 2 S.C. 5th Sumday toy at 10 am horse sick colic (Evacuated 24 horses)	W.E. Barnes
"	22.4.16		Visited 199th B.A.C. found reactions of 4 horses, to mallein test English method, had all 4 animals destroyed and found positive lesions in all cases. Lungs mostly being affected. Visited by D.D.V.S. Army, had a lengthy interview	W.E. Barnes
"	23.4.16		Visited Reg. toy, inspected horses, also D.A.C. Routine office work.	W.E. Barnes
"	24.4.16		Visited 174th Bde. R.F.A. inspected horses and B.A.C. which had been mallein'd. Routine office work.	W.E. Barnes
"	25.4.16		Visited 186th B.O.C. also 184th B.A.C. Routine office work.	W.E. Barnes
"	26.4.16		Visited Gloucester Regt & 225 Coy R.E. Routine office work	W.E. Barnes
"	27.4.16		Visited M.V.S. re evacuation of horses. Evacuated 5 horses & 2 mules	W.E. Barnes
"	28.4.16		Visited 199th B.A.C. and had a conference with Div V.O. in afternoon. Routine office work	W.E. Barnes
"	29.4.16		Visited 186th B.A.C. also M.V.S. Routine office work.	W.E. Barnes
"	30.4.16		Visited Div Rt. 9 horses and polide horses. Routine office work	W.E. Barnes

WAR DIARY
or
INTELLIGENCE SUMMARY
(Erase heading not required.)

Army Form C. 2118

Instructions regarding War Diaries and Intelligence Summaries are contained in F.S. Regs., Part II. and the Staff Manual respectively. Title Pages will be prepared in manuscript.

Place	Date	Hour	Summary of Events and Information	Remarks and references to Appendices
Locon	1.5.16		Visited M.V.S. & 174 & 179th Bde R.F.A. Visited Comm Coe 179th in the afternoon re Horses with Glanders, destroyed 6 horses and made P.M. all showed the Horses with Glanders reported the result to DDVS. Remainder of evening Glanders reported the result to DDVS. Routine office work	
	2.5.16		Visited 184th & 186th R.F.A. also D.A.C and sent out part of M M.P. reported on Routine office work	
"	3.5.16		Visited 179th Bde R.F.A. re testing of horses & M.V.S. Office work & met DDVS by appointment re Glanders case at the base	
"	4.5.16		Visited M.V.S. inspected Horses to be evacuated. 18 Horses 2 Mules. 2 Mare on Trek. Visited 39th Divn H.Q. Horses. Routine Office work	
"	5.5.16		Visited 179th B.A.C. retesting of Bay Horse with Roarks Glands. Visited 186th B.A.C. Conference with Vety Officers at 2.30. Destroyed Bay Mare 179th B.A.C. 3 Locomo found in lungs. Routine Office work	
"	6.5.16		Visited 50th M.V.S. went to D.D.V.S. office for mallein at Aire. Visited from the second time 179th B.A.C. Routine Office work	
"	7.5.16		Visited Horses 118th Infy Bde. & 179th B.A.C. went to conference at Aire Routine Office work	
"	8.5.16		Visited and inspected all horses in the 174th Bde R.F.A. & Routine Office work	
"	9.5.16		Visited and inspected all horses in the 179th Bde R.F.A. & B.A.C. inspected all horses in the 186th Bde R.F.A. Routine Office work	

W.E. Barrs Major A.V.C.
ADVS 39th Divn

ADVS 392A Vol 3

WAR DIARY
or
INTELLIGENCE SUMMARY
(Erase heading not required.)

Army Form C. 2118

Instructions regarding War Diaries and Intelligence Summaries are contained in F.S. Regs., Part II. and the Staff Manual respectively. Title Pages will be prepared in manuscript.

Place	Date	Hour	Summary of Events and Information	Remarks and references to Appendices
Govern	10.5.16		Went to La Gorgue to inspect horses arriving from Bonneuil. Met the 266th Coy A.O.C. to inspect horses. Met D.D.V.S. by appointment in the evening. Routine office work.	
	11.5.16		Visited Mobile Vety Sect to inspect horses for evacuation, evacuated 31 horses & 2 mules. 1 mare in foal. Inspected horses of the 184th Bde R.F.A. Met the A.A. & Q.M.G. with reference to horse standings. Routine office work.	
"	12.5.16		Visited the D.A.C. and 174th R.A.C. Weekly conference with Vety Officers. Had a message to meet the D.D.V.S. that day Re. inspection of 174th Bde. R.F.A. as the result of mentioning the matter to him on Wednesday, but received meeting him, waited at the Battery on the Brigade. Routine office work.	
"	13.5.16		Inspected the horses at Div. H.Q. Visited the 174th Bde. & O.C. 149th Bde and inspected all the horses. Routine office work.	
"	14.5.16		Visited 39th Sig Coy R.E. and inspected the horses. Inspected the horses 174th C Battery regarding shin disease, condemn of attainments of same. Arrears, and want of foot grooming. Routine office work.	
"	15.5.16		Visited the H.Q. of Artillery and inspected horses. Also the 186th Bde R.F.A. visited the units of the 118th Inf. Bde and inspected the horses. Routine office work.	

S.W. Barnes Major R.A.V.C.
ADVS 39th Div

1875 Wt. W593/826 1,000,000 4/15 J.B.C. & A. A.D.S.S./Forms/C. 2118.

Army Form C. 2118

WAR DIARY
or
INTELLIGENCE SUMMARY
(Erase heading not required.)

Instructions regarding War Diaries and Intelligence Summaries are contained in F. S. Regs., Part II. and the Staff Manual respectively. Title Pages will be prepared in manuscript.

Place	Date	Hour	Summary of Events and Information	Remarks and references to Appendices
Locon	16.5.16		Visited the 39th Divl. H.Q. and inspected the horses. Visited the various units of the 116th Infy. Bde. in afternoon. Routine office work.	
Locon	17.5.16		Inspected the horses of the 39th Div. Coy. R.E. went to the 50th M.V.S. to inspect the horses for evacuation, evacuated 81 horses. Very cases, and 1 Remount case. Mare in foal. Routine office work.	
"	18.5.16		Visited the 174th Bde. with reference to note from Lieut. R. Skelton A.V.C. who was unwell. Visited two batteries, and D.A.C.	
"	19.5.16		Notified the D.D.V.S. re. Lt. Skelton. visited the 174th Bde. R.F.A. and T.A.C. Had a conference with V.O. regarding the B.A.C.O. Routine office work. 8 p.m. visited the D.A.C. regarding a wire from O.C. Re a horse that was bad.	
"	20.5.16		Visited the 39th Divl. Hqrs horses, and H&grs. R.A. visited 39th D.A.C. and inspected the horses. Routine office work.	
"	21.5.16		Visited 39th Div. Coy R.E. and inspected the horses also the No 4 Coy. A.S.C. and 50th M.V.S. inspected the horses of the 184th Bde. R.F.A. with the V.O. in charge. Routine office work. W P Barnes Major AVC A.D.V.S. 39th Div	

Army Form C. 2118

WAR DIARY
or
INTELLIGENCE SUMMARY
(Erase heading not required.)

Instructions regarding War Diaries and Intelligence Summaries are contained in F. S. Regs., Part II. and the Staff Manual respectively. Title Pages will be prepared in manuscript.

Place	Date	Hour	Summary of Events and Information	Remarks and references to Appendices
Socx	22.5.16		Visited the D.A.C and inspected the horses also 179th. B.A.C with regard to the reorganisation of the Bde Amn Colms. Routine office work	LGB
"	23.5.16		Visited the 184th. Bde R.F.A and 186th R.F.A. with regard to the reorganisation and inspected all the horses and picked out the horses for details. Visited 39th H.Q. with regards to Amendments of surplus horses. Routine office work	
"	24.5.16		Visited the 50th M.V.S. and inspected horses for evacuation. evacuated 26 ft. 1.M. Vety cart. and 2 Remount. Base. Visited 39th Div. Sig. Coy R.E and inspected the horses. also the R.Q. Visited 39th. D.A.C and 179th Bde R.F.A Routine office work	
"	25.5.16		Visited the 118th Infy Battn. 116th Bn with V.O. and inspected the horses on the transport units. Visited the Details Horses and sent those not fit to travel to 50th M.V.S. Routine office work.	
"	26.5.16		Visited the horses of 39th H.Q. and the 117th Inf. Batt. and inspected the same. Had conference with V.O. at 2.30. Re. the reorganisation of the Amn. Colms. of the R.F.A. and redistribution of the V.O. Routine office work.	
"	27.5.16		Went by D.A.D.S. car. to 1st Army H.Q. with regard to Mullering of horses the some not reported to D.D.V.S. then return to city of Leut Shelton A.V.C Routine office work.	
"	28.5.16		Visited 97.V.S. also the 179th. Bde R.F.A. and inspected the horses. Routine office work. Inspected the Details horses before leaving for the Base. Met the D.D.V.S. by appointment with Re. Mullery of horses. Routine office work.	
"	29.5.16		Visited. G.C. 39th org. Boy R.E with reference to horse for etching. also the 116th Infy. Batt.	
"	30.5.16		Visited. 50th M.V.S. inspected horses for evacuation. evacuated. 34#. 8. 1 Mule. Routine office work	W G Barrett Lt Col AVS 39 Div
"	31.5.16			

WAR DIARY
or
INTELLIGENCE SUMMARY
(Erase heading not required.)

Army Form C. 2118

Instructions regarding War Diaries and Intelligence Summaries are contained in F. S. Regs, Part II. and the Staff Manual respectively. Title Pages will be prepared in manuscript.

ADVS 39 Div
Vol 4

Place	Date	Hour	Summary of Events and Information	Remarks and references to Appendices
1916 Locon	1·6·1916	—	Visited 179th R.F.A. & inspected horses also visited No 4 sub section DAC and inspected horses that had been mallained, – No 4 Section DAC. and inspected horses – general office work.	
"	June 2nd		Visited Mobile Vety section also visited 116th & 117th Inf Bdes with Vety Officers during afternoon. – general routine office work	
"	3rd		Visited Signal Coy Headquarters inspected horses, visited M.V.S. + 186th Bde R.F.A. general routine office work	
"	4th		Visited A & B Batteries 179th Brigade – general routine office work	
"	5th 6th		attended Yeomanry Conference held at Ayr.	
"	...		Visited M.V.S. 39th Sig Coy and A.S.C. also No 1 Section B.A.C. routine office work	
"	...		No 3 Section B.A.C. also visited M.V.S., 174th Bde R.F.A. general routine office work.	
"	7th		Visited O/C 50th M.V.S. to arrange about him taking change during my absence – general routine office work.	
"	8th		Visited No 4 Sect B.A.C & inspected horses, – visited No 3 Coy A.S.C.	
	9/6/16 to 16/6/16		Absent on leave	
"	16/6/16		Returned from leave & reported to DDVS 2nd Army	
"	17th		Visited 179th Bde R.F.A & inspected horses. general routine office work	
"	18th		– No 1 Coy A.S.C. & No 1 Coy D.A.C. and inspected horses general routine office work	
"	19th		Visited No 2 Coy A.S.C. inspected horses. – general routine office work	
"	20th		Visited 184th Brigade R.F.A. & 116th Inf Bde inspected horses general routine office work	

WAR DIARY
or
INTELLIGENCE SUMMARY
(Erase heading not required.)

Army Form C. 2118

Instructions regarding War Diaries and Intelligence Summaries are contained in F.S. Regs, Part II. and the Staff Manual respectively. Title Pages will be prepared in manuscript.

Place	Date	Hour	Summary of Events and Information	Remarks and references to Appendices
June. 1916	21st		Visited 184th Bde R.F.A. & No 3 Hy A.S.C. – visited M.V.S. & evacuated 23. to Base	
"	22nd		Visited 117th Inf Bde & No 4 Hy A.S.C. & inspected horses general routine office work.	
"	23rd		Inspected horses of No 2 Hy R.E. & No 2 Hy B.A.C.	
"	24th		Visited 225 Hy R.E. Held conference with Vety Officers of the Division re proposed inspection of horses in the Division. First Army Head-quarters of R.V.S. visited units under their change – inspection – visited Sec H. Section B.A.C. general routine office work	
"	25th		Visited 116th Inf Bde, 13th Gloucesters, 227th Hy Bty R.E. & No 3 Sec. B.A.C. & inspected horses – general routine office work.	
"	26th		M.A. D.R.V.S. 1st Army of Headquarters 39th Division 10 am and visited all the units in Division	
"	27th		MST DD VS. First Army at Headquarters 39th Division 10 am and visited commander of units in Division	
"	28th		Visited M.V.S. and inspected horses and evacuated 39. to Base general routine office work.	
"	29th		Visited 136th Heavy Battery & inspected horses – visited 174th Bde R.F.A., 117th Inf Bde & No 2 Sect. B.A.C. & inspected horses in each	
"	30th		Visited 50th M.V.S., also visited D.A.C. & inspected horses. Held conference with Veterinary Officers general routine office work	

39 / Vol 5

War Diary - July 1916

A.D.V.S.

WAR DIARY
or
INTELLIGENCE SUMMARY
(Erase heading not required.)

Army Form C. 2118

39th A.D.V.S.

Place	Date	Hour	Summary of Events and Information	Remarks and references to Appendices
Locon	1.7.1916	–	Visited 50th M.V.S. also visited 179th Bde R.F.A. 119th Inf Bde general routine office work.	Lt Col Barnes Inspector General passed thro'
	2.7.1916		Visited BQR-Q & 50th M.V.S. also visited No 2 Coy Divl Train, 118th Inf Bde 4 No 4 Section B.A.C. general routine office work.	
	3rd July		Visited M.V.S. also visited 186th Brigade R.F.A and inspected horses general routine office work.	
	4th		Visited No 3 Section BAC and inspected horses also visited 50th MVS. & general routine office work.	
	5th		Inspected M.M. Police horses and 39th Signal Coys horses also inspected horses for evacuation at 50th M.V.S.	
	6th		Inspected horses of No 4 Section BAC and two Batteries of R.F.A. (C 184th Bde & B 186th Bde). general routine office work.	
	7th		Visited 118th Infantry Bde & "C" Bty 186th Bde R.F.A. bombarde with V.O's general routine office work.	
	8th		Visited M.V.S. & G.H.Q. during afternoon moved to Bethune	
Bethune	9th		M.V.S moved to Bethune; visited G.H.Q. & 116th Inf Bde & inspected horses also inspected H.Q. horses. general routine office work.	
	10th		Visited 50th M.V.S. and G.H.Q. also visited 186th Bde (A Bty) with R.A 1st Field Remounts general routine office work.	
	11th		Visited No 1 Coy Divisional train also Cumberland Yeomanry, general routine office work.	
	12th		Visited G.H.Q., No 4 Coy Divl Train, 50th M.V.S, 1st Field Remounts, 1st Army 3gricls, No 3 Coy Divl Train also inspected 48 horses at 50th M.V.S. for evacuation general routine office work.	

Army Form C. 2118

WAR DIARY
or
INTELLIGENCE SUMMARY
(Erase heading not required.)

Instructions regarding War Diaries and Intelligence Summaries are contained in F. S. Regs., Part II. and the Staff Manual respectively. Title Pages will be prepared in manuscript.

Place	Date 1916	Hour	Summary of Events and Information	Remarks and references to Appendices
Bethune	13th July		Visited 174th Bde R.F.A., General H.Q. and 50th M.V.S. general routine office work	L/G Barns resuming A/D.S. & D.V.S.
	14th		Visited H.Q. SVO 1 & 2 Sections BAC, routine office work conference with Veterinary Officers.	
Locon	15th		Visited 50th M.V.S. and moved from Bethune to Locon.	
	16th		—"— E.H.Q., 50th M.V.S., and inspected horses of 179th Bde — 1814th Bde. general routine office work	
	17th		Inspected horses of No 3 Section BAC. also No 2 Section BAC conference from No 2 Section at H.Q. attended	
	18th		Visited No 2 Coy Divisional Train. also 132nd Field Amb. also general routine office work	
			M.Y.S., inspected horses of 179th Bde R.F.A. general routine office work	
			Visited horses in 116th Inf. Bde and 85.5th Bry R.E. general routine office work	
	19th		at 114th Inf Bde	
			Inspected horses of D.H.Q. and visited 50th M.V.S. & inspected 35 horses knew to evacuation. general routine office work	
	20th		Visited D.H.Q and 50th M.V.S. and inspected horses of 39th Signal Coy	
			also visited & inspected horses of 116th Inf. Bde. routine office work	
	21st		Visited D.H.Q. inspected horses of 179th Bde R.F.A. Field conference	
			with YO's general routine office work	
	22nd		Inspected horses of Westmorland & Cumberland Yeomanry (XI Corps Cavalry)	
			general routine office work	
	23rd		Visited D.H.Q. & 50th M.V.S. visited & inspected horses of 184th Bde R.F.A.	
			No 3 Coy Divisional Train and 134th Field Ambulance.	
	24th		Visited D.H.Q. R.F.A. & M.V.S. also inspected horses of 115th Inf Bde,	
			174th Bde R.F.A. & visited XI Corps Cavalry general routine office work	

WAR DIARY
or
INTELLIGENCE SUMMARY

(Erase heading not required.)

Army Form C. 2118

Instructions regarding War Diaries and Intelligence Summaries are contained in F.S. Regs., Part II. and the Staff Manual respectively. Title Pages will be prepared in manuscript.

Place	Date	Hour	Summary of Events and Information	Remarks and references to Appendices
Locon.	25.7.16		Visited D.H.Q. and 50th M.V.S. also No 1 & No 3. Sections D.A.C. and Divisional Signal Coy. general routine office work.	
	26.7.16		Visited 116th Inf Bde & inspected horses also visited D.T.Q. & 50th M.Y.S. & inspected 36. horses prior to evacuation. Inspected horses of 114th Bde R. & A. general routine office work.	
	27.7.16		Visited D.H.Q. & M.Y.S. Inspected horses of No 2. & 4. sections D.A.C. & No 3 Coy Divisional Train general routine office work.	
	28.7.16		Visited D.H.Q. & M.V.S. Inspected horses of 119th Bde (Inf). Conference with Vety Officers. Visited 114th & 119th Bdes R.F.A. inspected horses. general routine office work	
	29.7.16		Visited D.H.Q. and 50th M.V.S. Inspected horses of 179th & 181st Bdes R. & A. general routine office work	
	30.7.16		Visited D.H.Q. & M.V.S. also visited No 3 Coy Divisional Train general routine office work.	
	31.7.16		Visited D.H.Q. & M.V.S. general routine office work. Inspected horses of Divisional R.A.	

W G Barnes
Major AVC
ADVS.
39th Division

WAR DIARY or INTELLIGENCE SUMMARY

Army Form C. 2118

Instructions regarding War Diaries and Intelligence Summaries are contained in F.S. Regs., Part II. and the Staff Manual respectively. Title Pages will be prepared in manuscript.

(Erase heading not required.)

Place	Date	Hour	Summary of Events and Information	Remarks and references to Appendices
Lozon	1/7/1914		Visited 50th M.Y.S. also visited 179th Bde R.F.A., 117th Inf Bde & No 2 Section D.A.C. General routine office work	
	2 -"-		Visited BHQ & 50th MYS also visited No 2 Coy Divl Train, 118th Inf Bde and No 4 Sectn D.A.C. — general routine office work.	
	3 -"-		Visited M.Y.S, 186th Bde R.F.A. inspected horses general routine office work	
	4 -"-		Visited No 3 Sectn D.A.C. & inspected horses also visited 50th M.Y.S. general routine office work.	
	5 -"-		Inspected Divisional Bde. horses. 39th Signal Coys horses and 50 horses at 50th M.Y.S. prior to evacuation. General routine office work.	
	6 -"-		Inspected horses at "B" (186th Bde) & two Batteries of R.F.A. ("C" 184th Bde & "B" 186th Bde).	
	7 -"-		Visited 118th Inf Bde, 50th M.Y.S. & "C" Bty 186th Bde R.F.A. general routine office work.	
Bethune	8 -"-		Field conference with Y.O's at Bethune with 1st 2nd Q.	
	9 -"-		Visited LofC YM.Y.S. moved to Bethune. Visited LHQ 416th Inf Bde & inspected horses also inspected RSHQ horses.	
	10 -"-		Visited M.Y.S. + D. H.Q., 186th Bde (A Bty) with R.A. 1st Field remounts general routine office work	
	11 -"-		Visited No 1 Coy Divl Train, 50th M.Y.S. & Westmorland & Cumberland Yeomanry general routine office work	
	12 -"-		Visited G.H.Q. No 4 Coy Divl Train + inspected 48 horses at 50th M.Y.S. 1st Field Remounts 1st Army prior to evacuation	
	13 -"-		Visited 174th Bde R.F.A. BHQ & 50th M.Y.S. general routine office work.	
	14 -"-		Visited BHQ, No 1 & 2 Sectn D.A.C. general routine office work.	
Lozon	15 -"-		Visited 50th M.Y.S. and moved BHQ from Bethune to Lozon. Conference with Y.O/o	

JBBarnes
Major R.A.
39th A.D.V.S.
2nd Divn

WAR DIARY
or
INTELLIGENCE SUMMARY
(Erase heading not required.)

Army Form C. 2118

Instructions regarding War Diaries and Intelligence Summaries are contained in F.S. Regs., Part II. and the Staff Manual respectively. Title Pages will be prepared in manuscript.

Place	Date	Hour	Summary of Events and Information	Remarks and references to Appendices
Lozeau	16.9.16		Visited BHQ. 50th M.V.S. & inspected horses of 179th Bde & 184th Bde, — general routine office work. Inspected horses of No 3 Sectn DAC, No 2 Sectn DAC, visited No 2 Coy Divl Train, attended conference at BHQ.	
	17-11-			
	18-11-		Visited M.V.S., - inspected horses at 132nd Field Ambulance, at 119th Inf Bde & 255 Bny R.E. general routine office work.	
	19-11-		Inspected horses at HQ.; - visited 50th M.V.S. & inspected 35 horses prior to evacuation. general routine office work.	
	20-11-		Visited BHQ. & 50th M.V.S. inspected horses 39th Signal Coy, 4116th Inf Bde, routine office work.	
	21-11-		Visited BHQ: inspected horses of 179th Bde R.F.A. held conference with Vety Officers. general routine office work.	
	22-11-		Inspected horses of Westmoreland & Cumberland Yeomanry (XI Corps Cavalry) general routine office work	
	23-11-		Visited BHQ & 50th M.V.S. inspected horses of 184th R.F.A. No 3 Coy Divl Train 134th Fd Ambce.	
	24-11-		Visited BHQ. & M.V.S. inspected horses at 118th Inf Bde, 174th Bde R.F.A. XI Corps Cavalry general routine office work.	
	25-11-		Visited D.H.Q & 50th M.V.S also No 1 & 3 Sectns DAC. & Divl Signal Coy, — general routine office work	
	26-11-		Visited 116th Inf Bde & inspected horses, also visited BHQ & 50th M.V.S. & inspected 36 horses prior to being evacuated — inspected horses of 174th Bde R.F.A. general routine office work.	
	27-11-		Visited BHQ & 50th M.V.S. Inspected horses of No 2 & 4 Sectns DAC & No 3 Coy Divl Train general routine office work.	
	28-11-		Visited BHQ. & M.V.S., 119th Inf Bde, 174th, 179th Bdes R.F.A. & inspected horses. Conference with Vety Officers. general routine office work.	
	29-11-		Visited BHQ & M.V.S. inspected horses of 179th & 1821st Bdes R.F.A. general routine office work.	
	30-11-		Visited BHQ & M.V.S, No 3. Coy Divl Train general routine office work.	
	31-11-		Visited BHQ & M.V.S. & inspected horses of 39th Divn R.A. general routine office work	

EJBains
Major A.V.S.
39th Div.

WAR DIARY
or
INTELLIGENCE SUMMARY
(Erase heading not required.)

Army Form C. 2118

Instructions regarding War Diaries and Intelligence Summaries are contained in F.S. Regs., Part II. and the Staff Manual respectively. Title Pages will be prepared in manuscript.

Place	Date	Hour	Summary of Events and Information	Remarks and references to Appendices
Rouen	16.9.'16		Visited BHQ. 50th M.Y.S. & inspected horses of 179th Bde & 184th Bde,— general routine office work	39th ADVS Div
	17-11-		Inspected horses of No 3 Sectn BAC, No 2 Sectn BAC, Visited No 2 Coy Div Train, attended conference at BHQ	
	18-11-		Visited M.V.S., — Inspected horses at 132nd Field Ambulance, at 117th Inf Bde & 255 Coy R.E. general routine office work.	
	19-11-		Inspected horses at HQ; — Visited 50th M.Y.S. — inspected 35 horses prior to evacuation general routine office work	
	20-11-		Visited BHQ. & 50th M.Y.S.: inspected horses 39th Signal Coy, 4/16th Inf Bde, routine office work	
	21-11-		Visited BHQ:— inspected horses of 179th Bde BHQ R.F.A. field conference with Vety officers general routine office work	
	22-11-		Inspected horses of Westmoreland & Cumberland Yeomanry (XI Corps Cavalry) general routine office work	
	23-11-		Visited BHQ & 50th M.Y.S inspected horses of 184th Inf Bde, 134th & 3rd Ambee. No 3 Coy Div Train XI Corps Cavalry	
	24-11-		Visited BHQ, & M.Y.S. inspected horses at 118th Inf Bde, 174th Bde R.F.A. general routine office work.	
	25-11-		Visited DHQ. & 50th M.Y.S. also No 1 & 3 Sectns BAC & Divl Signal Coy,— general routine office work	
	26-11-		Visited 116th Inf Bde & inspected horses, also visited BHQ & 50th M.V.S. & inspected 36 horses prior to being evacuated — inspected horses of 174th Bde R.F.A. general routine office work.	
	27-11-		Visited BHQ, & 50th M.Y.S. inspected horses of No 2 & 4 Sectns BAC & No 3 Coy Divl Train general routine office work	
	28-11-		Visited BHQ, & M.Y.S., 117th Inf Bde, 174 & 179th Bdes R.F.A. inspected horses. Conference with Vety Officers general routine office work	
	29-11-		Visited BHQ & M.Y.S.	
	30-11-		Visited BHQ & M.V.S, No 3 Coy Divl Train inspected horses of 179 & 184th Bdes R.F.A. general routine office work	
	31-11-		Visited BHQ. M.Y.S. & inspected horses of 39th Divn R.A. general routine office work	

1375 Wt. W593/826 1,000,000 4/15 J.B.C. & A. A.D.S.S./Forms/C. 2118.

WAR DIARY or INTELLIGENCE SUMMARY

Army Form C. 2118

39 / August

ADVS V86

Place	Date	Hour	Summary of Events and Information	Remarks and references to Appendices
Locon	1/8/16		Visited 50th M.V.S., 39th Divisional animals. Shown & 174th Bde R.F.A. & inspected general routine office work.	
	2nd		Visited 50th M.V.S., 115th Infantry Bde, 39th B.A.C. general routine office work.	
	3rd		Visited 50th M.V.S., 39th Divisional train, inspected 39th animals at 50th MVS prior to evacuation and 116th Infantry Bde, & inspected horses.	Divisional Headqrs
	4th		Visited 50th M.V.S., also inspected horses of 134th Fd Ambce, R.E's & general routine office work.	
	5th		Visited 50th M.V.S., 117th Infantry Bde. Inspected horses of D.H.Q. 119th & 184th Bde R.F.A. also visited MVS & inspected general routine office work.	
	6th		Visited 50th M.V.S. Held conference with DDVS. 1st Army general routine office work.	
	7th		Inspected horses of three Companies of 39th Divisional Train. Visited 50th general routine office work.	
	8th		MVS & DHQ general routine office work.	
	9th		Visited 50th M.V.S. three sections B.A.C., 134th Field Ambce & RE's general routine office work.	
	10th		Visited 50th M.V.S., 116th Inf Bde, 119th Inf Bde, & D.H.Q. general routine office work.	
	11th		Visited 50th M.V.S. & inspected 34 horses prior to evacuation. 186th & 184th Bde R.F.A. + D.H.Q. general routine office work.	
	12th		Visited 133rd Field Ambce, 134th Field Ambce, 117th Bde R.F.A., 234th Coy RE general routine office work.	
Roellecourt	13th		Divisional Headquarters moved from Locon to Roellecourt. Visited 50th M.V.S. Reported to DDVS. Third Army. Visited 39th BHQ.	
	14th		General routine office work.	
	15th		Visited & inspected horses of 119th & 184th Bde R.F.A. & 39th B.A.C. Visited 39th BAC. general routine office work.	
	16th		Visited 132nd Field Ambce, 116th Bde R.F.A & D.H.Q. general routine office work.	
	17th		Visited 50th M.V.S, 39th B.A.C., 116th Inf Bde R.F.A. & 133rd Fd Ambce. general routine office work.	

WAR DIARY
or
INTELLIGENCE SUMMARY
(Erase heading not required.)

Army Form C. 2118

Instructions regarding War Diaries and Intelligence Summaries are contained in F. S. Regs., Part II. and the Staff Manual respectively. Title Pages will be prepared in manuscript.

Place	Date Aug.	Hour	Summary of Events and Information	Remarks and references to Appendices
Rocquecourt	17th		Visited 179th Bde R.F.A., 186th Bde R.F.A. & D.A.C. also visited 116th Inf Bde general routine office work.	
	18th		Inspected horses at 50th M.V.S. prior to being evacuated. Visited 184th Inf Bde R.F.A. 117th Inf Bde & 50th Q general routine office work.	
	19th		Visited Railhead & inspected 60 remounts. Visited 134th Fld Ambce	
	20th		4TH Q. general routine office work.	
	21st		Visited 26th Coy A.S.C., R.F.A. H.Q. & 179th Bde R.F.A. Visited D.A.C. re distribution of remounts.	
	22nd		Visited 50th M.V.S., 174th Bde R.F.A. & D.A.C. Inspected horses of Bde R.A. before moving into new area. Visited 50th Q routine office work	
	23rd		Visited 50th M.V.S. 2nd inspected 141 animals prior to evacuation.	
	24th		Visited D.H.Q. & inspected H.Q. horses, general routine office work.	
			Moved with DHQ from Rocquecourt to Bus. general routine office work.	
Bus.	25th		Visited 179th Bde R.F.A. on the move. Also Bus Train, general routine office work	
	26th		Visited 50th M.V.S. & St Leger. & D.A.C. at Orville, were visited by BSVS general routine office work.	
	27th		Visited M.V.S. Inspected horses of 184th & 186th Bde R.F.A. moved from Bus to Achiena with D.H.Q.	
Achiena	28th		Visited M.V.S. Inspected horses of Div Train. general routine office work.	
	29th		Visited M.V.S. Inspected horses 179th Bde R.F.A., proceeded to Doullens re horse left by 119th M.G Coy general routine office work.	
	30th		Visited M.V.S. Proceeded to Railhead to inspect remounts arrived. Visited DAC + 174th Bde R.F.A. suspect influenza (mild form) Visited No 4 Sdn. DAC, DHQ + general routine office work	
	31st		Visited M.V.S. inspected 29 horses for evacuation to No 7 Vety Hospital, routine office work Proceeded to 116th Inf Bde position re horses killed by shell fire.	

L.E.Barnes
ADVS 39th Div

WAR DIARY or INTELLIGENCE SUMMARY

Army Form C. 2118

ADVS 39
ADVS 39 39/7
Vol 7

Place	Date	Hour	Summary of Events and Information	Remarks and references to Appendices
Advance	1/9/16	—	Inspected horses of B.A.C. and 184th Brigade R.F.A. officers of 39th Division.	
	2nd		Visited Vety offices XI Divn. MVS. Inspected 57th & 58th & 59th & 60th & 133rd Bde.R.F.A. artillery & inspected advanced collecting station. Routine office work.	
	3rd		Proceeded to advance collecting post 4am. Visited various units during the day & returned 8pm.	
	4th		Visited by D.D.V.S. Visited M.V.S. Inspected horses of B.A.C. at Orville. also visited Div trains. General routine office work.	
	5th		Visited 50th M.V.S. 179th, 186th Bde R.H.A. Visited No 5 Field Ambce. re contractions	
	6th		Visited M.V.S. 117th Inf Bde. – general routine office work. Inspected 50th MVS & MT 110 & Bde general	
	7th		Visited M.V.S. 184th Brigade. Inspected Headqts Bde. general routine office work.	
	8th		Inspected horses of 252 Tunly Coy, 50th MVS & 174th Tunly Coy. Visited 2nd Army (Siege) R.E. & 6th Labour Coy R.E. conference with YOs.	
	9th		Visited 50th M.V.S. Inspected horses of 186th Bde R.F.A. received about MVS work inspected it Rwmh from DDVS Reserve Army, general routine office work. Horses inspected.	
	10th		Inspected horses of 89th Divnmnal Train & 50th M.V.S. routine office work	
	11th		Inspected horses of 39th D.A.C. Visited 50th MVS. routine "	
	12th		Visited M.V.S. Inspected horses of 179th Bde R.F.A. visited by DDVS Res Army to inspect remounts.	
	13th		Visited MVS. Inspected 16 horses prior to evacuation. Visited 116th & 116th Inf Bde. general routine office work	
	14th		Visited M.V.S. inspected horses of 6th Labour & 2nd Siege Bny, 174th Bde R.E. general routine office work	
	15th		Visited MVS & 39th BAC. 117th Inf Bde. held conference with YOs. general routine office work	
	16th		Visited MVS inspected 38 horses prior to evacuation. General routine office work	

WAR DIARY
or
INTELLIGENCE SUMMARY
(Erase heading not required.)

Army Form C. 2118

Place	Date	Hour	Summary of Events and Information	Remarks and references to Appendices
Acheux	17th		Visited M.V.S., 174th & 186th Bde R.F.A. general routine office work.	T.E.Barnshaw?
	18th		" " 179th & 184th " "	
	19th		" " 39th D.A.C. 174th Bde R.F.A. general routine office work	
	20th		" inspected 24 horses prior to evacuation & 2nd Sange Coy R.E. general routine office work.	
	21st		Visited M.V.S., 118th Inf Bde., 174th Bde. R.F.A. 252nd Coy R.E. 6th Seaforth Regt. Visited Railroad & inspected remounts; 2 A.F.C. officers arrived	
	22nd		Conference with Veterinary Officers	
	23rd		Visited M.V.S. inspected 30 horses prior to evacuation; visited 174th & 184th & 186th Bdes R.F.A. with new Vety Officer. routine office work	
	24th		Visited 39th D.A.C. & inspected horses for W.D. purposes. visited 50th M.Y.S. general routine office work	
	25th		Visited 119th Inf Bde & 186th Bde R.F.A. visited M.V.S. routine office work	
	26th		Visited 179th & 184th Bdes R.F.A. visited D.A.C. & M.V.S. "	
	27th		Visited M.V.S. inspected 54 horses prior to evacuation, Visited 174th Sunly Coy & Pack Train inspected new standings. visited M.V.S.	
	28th		Visited M.V.S., inspected horses of 3rd D.A.C. 116th Inf Bde. routine office work.	
	29th		Visited M.V.S. inspected horses. visited 174th & 252nd Sunly Coys. held conference with vety officers general routine office work	
	30th		Visited M.V.S. inspected 3q. horses prior to evacuation. visited D.A.C. 174th & 179th Bde R.F.A.	

WAR DIARY or INTELLIGENCE SUMMARY

(Erase heading not required.)

Army Form C. 2118

ADVS 39th Vol 8

Place	Date 1916	Hour	Summary of Events and Information	Remarks and references to Appendices
Acheux	Oct 1st	—	Visited 50th MVS, 174th Bde RFA, 179th Bde RFA, and 184th Bde RFA and inspected animals; general routine office work.	
"	2nd	—	Moved with Divisional Headquarters to Hedauville.	
Hedauville	3rd	—	Visited 50th M.V.S. & inspected 22 animals prior to evacuation, inspected animals of 39th D.A.C. & Divisional Train; 39 D.A.C. routine office work.	
"	4th	—	Inspected horses of Divisional Headquarters & 50th M.V.S.	
"	5th	—	Visited 50th MVS & inspected 14 horses prior to evacuation, visited Gloucester Regt & 20th Cheshire Labour Batt. & inspected horses.	
"	6th	—	Visited MVS office work.	
"	7th	—	Visited MVS & inspected animals of 117th Inf Bde. Bde conference with Vety officer; general routine office work.	
Bouzincourt	—	—	Moved Divisional Headquarters to Bouzincourt; visited and inspected horses at 50th MVS also inspected 38 animals prior to evacuation; visited 156 Bde RFA + Y.O /c 24th Heavy Arty.	
Bouzincourt	8th	—	Visited 50th MVS & inspected animals of 132nd Fld Amb.	
"	9th	—	Visited 39th DAC & 50th MVS; inspected horses of 133rd Fld Amb. routine office work.	
"	10	—	Visited 225th Fld Amb, RE, 15th Divisional Artillery; inspected horses of attached Heavy Arty, & 20th Cheshire Labour Batt. + inspected animals - general routine office work.	
"	11	—	Visited MVS: inspected 64 animals prior to evacuation.	
"	12	—	Visited MVS: inspected horses with Y Off. /c 18th Heavy Arty & 39th Siege Batty RE 39th Rive Train, held conference with Y.O. & 39th DAC + 179th Bde RFA. held conference inspected horses of 39th DAC. + 179th Bde RFA. general routine office work.	
"	13	—	Visited Yety office routine office work.	
"	14	—	Visited 50th MVS inspected 31 animals prior to evacuation. Visited 184th Bde R.F.A. general routine office work.	

J.E.Burns

WAR DIARY or INTELLIGENCE SUMMARY

Army Form C. 2118

Place	Date 1916	Hour	Summary of Events and Information	Remarks and references to Appendices
Burguegrand	Oct 15th		Visited 50th M.V.S., 118th Inf Bde nursed & inspected animals of Heedam R.E. general office work.	L.G. Burns msgs A.V.C. R. Div 8 39th Divn
"	16th		Visited 50th M.V.S., 117th Inf Bde, 134th Fld Amb & 20th Cheshire Regt, also inspected H.Q., 134th Inf Bde, 117th Bde horses	
"	17th		Visited M.V.S., A.S.C. with O.C. Divnal Train. Inspected horses for shunt by 50th M.V.S. & inspected 116 Inf Bde, general routine office work	
"	18th		Visited 50th M.V.S., 83rd Bde, 16th Div Arty, general routine office work	
"	19th		Visited 50th M.V.S., inspection of animals of 114 Bde R.F.A. visited H.Q. 39 R.A.C. + inspection of horses of 174 Bde R.F.A., general routine office work	
"	20th		Visited M.V.S. 118th Inf Bde visited horses; routine office work	
"	21st		Reunion D.D.V.S., 118th & 114 Bde R.F.A.'s general routine vety offrs, routine office work	
"	22nd		Visited M.V.S. & inspected 16 animals prior to evacuation inspected D.A.Q. animals injured by shellfire visited 116th Bde R.F.A.	Lt
"	23rd		Visited 114 Bde R.F.A., 8 animals inspected prior to evacuation general routine office work	
"	24th		Visited M.V.S., 133rd Field Amb; 118th Inf Bde; general routine office work	
"	25th		" " 149 Bde R.F.A. + 39th R.F.C. general routine office work	
"	26th		Visited M.V.S., inspected 30 animals prior to evacuation, visited 152 & 134 Fld Ambulances, general routine office work	
"	27th		Visited M.V.S., 227 + 234 Fld Coy R.E.'s general routine office work	
"	28th		" " 118th Inf Bde, 186 Bde R.F.A., field conference with vet officers	
"			116 + 119 Infantry Bde, visited by Div 3 Reserve Army. Inspected 21 animals in M.V.S. prior to evacuation routine office work	
"	29th		Visited M.V.S., A.S.C. & 174 Bde R.F.A. general routine office work	
"	30th		Visited 50th M.V.S. & 39th D.A.C. general routine office work remounts arrived	
"	31st		Visited M.V.S. routine office work & inspected remounts arrived	

WAR DIARY or INTELLIGENCE SUMMARY

Army Form C. 2118

A.D.V.S. 39th Division

Place	Date Nov 1916	Hour	Summary of Events and Information	Remarks
Bouzincourt	1st		Visited M.V.S. inspected general routine office work.	
"	2nd		Visited & inspected animals 116 & 117 Inf Bdes, 13th Gloucesters & 20 Cheshires	
"	3rd		Inspected animals 184 & 186 Bdes R.F.A, 133 Field Ambulance general routine office work.	
"	4th		Held conference with veterinary officers R.F.A.	
"	5th		Visited M.V.S. inspected horses of 225, 227, & 234 Field coys R.E.	
"	6th		Inspected horses of 116 & 118 Infantry Brigade general routine office work	
"	6th		Inspected 63 animals at M.V.S. tabor Brigade & M.V.S. routine office work	
"	7th		Inspected horses of 114 Infantry Brigade general routine office work	
"	8th		Inspected horses 174 & 179 Bdes R.F.A	
"	9th		Visited M.V.S. inspected 64 horses prior to evacuation; inspected animals of R.F.C. & Artillery horses in rest area, routine office work.	
"	9th		Visited M.V.S. & inspected 28 animals prior to evacuation. Visited 132 & 134 Field Amb. - 30% Casuals. general routine office work.	
"	10th		Visited M.V.S. & inspected 69 animals prior to evacuation; inspected horses F. 117 Inf Bdes, 225, 227, 234 Field coys. boys conference with vety officers	
"	11th		Visited & M.V.S. inspected 32 animals prior to evacuation inspected animals 116 Inf Bde & 13 Gloucesters general routine office work.	
"	12th		Inspected animals 184 & 186 Bdes R.F.A. general routine office work.	
"	13th		Inspected horses of 174 & 179 Bdes R.F.A. general routine office work	
"	14th		Visited M.V.S. A.S.C. general routine office work	
"	15th		Visited M.V.S. inspected 39 animals prior to evacuation office work	
"	16th		Visited R.F.C. & animals put into rest area, routine office work. waited 114 & Inf Bde	
"	16th		Moved with Divisional Headqrs from Bouzincourt to Boisleux, met remounds at Acheux.	
Bouzincourt / Hazebrouck	17th		Moved from Bouzincourt to Hazebrouck.	
Hazebrouck	18th		Moved from Hazebrouck to Coquelleaq; arranged office billet.	

Army Form C. 2118

WAR DIARY

~~INTELLIGENCE SUMMARY~~

(Erase heading not required.)

A.D.V.S. 30th Division

Instructions regarding War Diaries and Intelligence Summaries are contained in F. S. Regs., Part II. and the Staff Manual respectively. Title Pages will be prepared in manuscript.

Place	Date	Hour	Summary of Events and Information	Remarks and references to Appendices
Esquelbecq	November 1916			
	19th		Arranged sites for M.V.S: general routine office work	
"	20th		Visited Hazebrouck re reported animal to D.D.V.S. 2nd Army. Visited 116 I.F. Bde. general routine office work.	
"	21st		Visited M.V.S: inspected horses of Headqr. Signal Co. visited 118th Inf. Bde. general routine office work.	
"	22nd		Visited M.V.S. to 2 Coy A.S.C. b/ Cheshires & Cambridgeshires. general routine office work.	
"	23rd		Visited A.D.V.S. inspected theodr. animals. routine office work	
"	24th		Held conference with veterinary officers 90 M.V.S. carrying on during absence. routine office work.	
"	25th		general routine office work.	
"	26th		Visited D.D.V.S. 2nd Army general routine office work.	
"	27th		general routine office work.	
"	28th		Inspected 16 animals prior to evacuation routine office work.	
"	29th		Visited Vety. Officers of Artillery units re reorganization of Rdes.	
"	30th		Visited 116th & 118th Inf. Bdes also 2 Coy's Divl. Train. general routine office work.	

W. W. Buchanan Capt. A.V.C.
for A.D.V.S. 30th Div.

WAR DIARY
or
INTELLIGENCE SUMMARY

(Erase heading not required.)

Army Form C. 2118

Vol 10
A.D.V.S. 39th Division

Place	Date	Hour	Summary of Events and Information	Remarks and references to Appendices
	December 1916			
Bequerez	1st		Visited 116th Inf. Bde. "13th Glosters inspected animals of latter unit." Field conference with Bdy. Officer.	A.D.V.S. on leave work carried on by O/C 50th M.V.S.
	2nd		Visited 39th D.M.C. & inspected animals. general routine office work.	
	3rd		Inspected 22 animals at 50th M.V.S. prior to evacuation. general routine office work	
	4th		Visited 179th Bde. R.F.A. inspected horses general routine office work	
	5th		Inspected 18 animals of 50th M.V.S. prior to evacuation. general office work (A.D.V.S. returned off leave)	
	6th		Inspected 23 animals at 50th M.V.S. prior to evacuation. visited 118th Bde. + inspected horses.	
	7th		Visited M.V.S. visited No 1. Coy R.E. routine office work	
	8th		Visited M.V.S. Veterinary Stables inspected animals of A Bty 174, 176 Bde R.F.A. field conference with 116 + 118 Inf. Bdes.	
	9th		Visited M.V.S. inspected horses of A.S.C. general routine office work.	
	10th		Visited general office and Nos. 243 Coy A.S.C. general routine office work, visited M.V.S. and inspected 39 animals prior to evacuation.	
	11th			
	12th		D.A.C. and 1 Coy A.S.C. general routine office work. Visited M.V.S. inspected 4 horses prior to evacuation. Visited 174th Bde, 176th Bde. R.F.A. routine office work	
	13th		2nd Army and inspected 30 animals prior to evacuation, visited 39 Div. Visited M.V.S. inspected horses. general routine office work.	
	14th		Moved with Headqrs. to St Sixte. routine office work.	
St Sixte	15th		Visited 179th Bde. R.F.A. field conference with Vety. Officers general routine office work.	
	16th		Visited M.V.S. and inspected horses of 133, 134 Fld. Amb. routine office work.	
	17th		Visited M.V.S. also 227 + 225 Field Coys R.E. routine office work.	

B.B.James
Major R.V.C.
A.D.V.S. 39 Div.

Army Form C. 2118

WAR DIARY
or
INTELLIGENCE SUMMARY
(Erase heading not required.)

ADVS 39th Division

Instructions regarding War Diaries and Intelligence Summaries are contained in F.S. Regs., Part II. and the Staff Manual respectively. Title Pages will be prepared in manuscript.

Place	Date	Hour	Summary of Events and Information	Remarks and references to Appendices
St Souhe	December 1916			
	18th		Visited M.V.S. inspected horses of 186th Bde R.F.A. general routine office work.	
	19th		Visited M.V.S. inspected 11 animals prior to evacuation, inspected animals of 117 Inf Bde & 13th Gloucesters, general routine office work.	
	20th		Visited M.V.S. inspected horses of 179 Bde R.F.A. & 116 Inf Bde general routine office work.	
	21st		Inspected animals of 174 Bde R.F.A. & 118 Inf Bde routine office work.	
	22nd		Inspected animals of 23rd Fd Coy R.E. held conference with Vety Officers general routine office work.	
	23rd		Inspected horses of Divisional Train. visited M.V.S.	
	24th		Visited 13th Gloster, 225 Field Coy R.E. and M.V.S. general routine office work.	
	25		Visited 50th M.V.S. inspected horses of 174 Bde R.F.A.	
	26th		Visited 50th M.V.S. general routine office work.	
	27th		Visited 50th M.V.S. inspected 23 animals prior to evacuation, inspected 133 & 134 Field Ambs general routine office work.	
	28th		Inspected animals of 117 Inf Bde & 39th DAC visited M.V.S. general routine office work.	
	29th		Visited 50th M.V.S. took charge of M.V.S. during OC's absence on leave, inspected animals 221 Field Coy R.E. routine office work.	
	30th		Visited M.V.S. inspected horses of H.Q. Bde R.F.A. & 186 Bde R.F.A. held conference with Vety Officers general routine office work.	
	31st		Visited M.V.S. & 118th Inf Bde inspected horses of Divisional Train general routine office work.	
			Visited M.V.S. visited inspected horses of 10th Entrenching Battalion general routine office work.	

WAR DIARY
or
INTELLIGENCE SUMMARY
(Erase heading not required.)

Army Form C. 2118

A.D.V.S. 39th Division

E E Barnes
Lt Col 24/1/18

Place	Date	Hour	Summary of Events and Information	Remarks and references to Appendices
St Sixthe	January 1919.			
	1st		Visited 50th M.V.S. inspected animals Divisional M.M.P., 225 R.B, 186 Bde RFA	
"	2nd		Visited 50th M.V.S. + inspected 49 animals prior to evacuation	
"	3rd		Divl Salvage Coy. and 39th RMC general routine office work	
"	4th		Visited 50th M.V.S. inspected horses 133 + 134 Fld Amb. Band 117 Inf Bde	
"	5th		general routine office work.	
"	5th		Visited M.V.S., inspected animals 179 Bde R.F.A., 13th Gloucesters.	
"	6th		general routine office work; Veterinary Officers inspected animals	
"	6th		Held conference with Sectn DAC. routine office work	
"	7th		114 Bde R.F.A. and No. 4 Sectn DAC.	
"	7th		Visited 50th M.V.S. visited BDVS. 2nd Army, inspected horses	
"	8th		10th Buckinghams Battalion, routine office work visited Div Train	
"	8th		Visited M.V.S. inspected animals 116 Inf Bde routine office work.	
"	9th		general routine office work.	
"	9th		Inspected animals at 132 Field Amb. RHQ + 38 Div Schools	
"	10th		visited M.V.S., general routine office work.	
"	10th		Visited M.V.S. + inspected 53 animals prior to evacuation.	
"	11th		Visited R.34 Bery R.B, 13 Glosters, 186 Bde RFA routine office work.	
"	11th		visited 14th Bde R.F.A; visited by BDVS 2nd Army.	
"	12th		general routine office work.	
"	12th		Visited 179 Bde RFA, 118th Inf Bde + 50th M.V.S. routine office work	
"	12th		Held conference with veterinary Officers. visited 117 Inf Bde	
"	13th		229 Bery R.G. and 1 Sectn 39 DAC. general routine office work.	
"	13th		Visited 50th M.V.S. visited new area on movement M.V.S. office	
"	14th		general routine office work.	
"	14th		Visited 116 Inf Bde + M.V.S. Visited BDVS. general routine office work	
"	15th		Moved with Divl Headqrs to Poperinghe.	
Poperinghe	16th		Visited 50th M.V.S. inspected 15 animals prior to evacuation visited	
			DAC + A/114 + 4/18 + 4/181 R.F.A. general routine office work.	

WAR DIARY
or
INTELLIGENCE SUMMARY

(Erase heading not required.)

Army Form C. 2118

Vol XI
ADYS 39th Division

Place	Date 1917	Hour	Summary of Events and Information	Remarks and references to Appendices
Poperinghe	Jan 17th		Visited 50th M.V.S. inspected horses 179 Bde R.F.A. 133 Fld Amb attended conference with DDVS 2nd Army general routine office work.	
"	18th		Inspected horses of M.V.S., AMB Bhqs 186 Bde, Dip Bath, Stone Rift Bath, general routine office work.	
"	19th		Held conference with D.V. Officer. visited 2/1 Northern R.B. & Horse Poperinghe Bath general routine office work.	
"	20th		Visited M.V.S., 13th Gloucesters 133, 132 Fld Amb. routine office work.	
"	21st		Inspected animals M.V.S., 186 Bde R.F.A. 134 Fld Amb general routine office work.	
"	22nd		Visited 50th M.V.S. & inspected 19 animals prior to evacuation. Stone Rift Bath. general routine office work	
"	23rd		Visited 50th M.V.S. & Div Headqrs & C.R.A. inspected Horse Rail Train general routine office work.	E.B. Benno 22/2/32?
"	24th		Visited 50th M.V.S., Div H.Q. re mange. Inspected horses at 186 Bde R.F.A. 6/14th & 6/14th Bde R.F.A., Div Signals, 118 Inf Bde. routine office work	
"	25th		Visited M.V.S. inspected animals 225 horse R.E. routine office work.	
"	26th		— " — Div Train — Supply Officer 8th Corps. routine office work.	
"	27th		Visited 39 D.A.C. 4 2 Sections D.A.C. general routine office work.	
"	28th		Visited M.V.S., 186 Bde R.F.A., 118th Inf Bde. & 229 Co R.E routine office work.	
"	29th		Visited M.V.S. 114th Bde R.F.A., Headqrs Division & 8th Corps Dip: interviewed A.D.V.S. 8th Corps general routine office work.	
"	30th		Inspected animals at 50th M.V.S., visited 8th Corps Dip interviewed D.A.Q.M.G. 8th Corps re programme for Dip routine office work.	
"	31st		Visited Rfte Q. & M.V.S.; superintended Dipping of horse at Dipping Bath. general routine office work.	Major A.V.C. ADVS 39- Division

WAR DIARY
INTELLIGENCE SUMMARY
(Erase heading not required.)

Army Form C. 2118

Vol 12
A.D.V.S. 39 Division

L.E. Barnes
Major
A.D.V.S. 39 Division.

Place	Date	Hour	Summary of Events and Information	Remarks and references to Appendices
Poperinghe	Feb 1st 1917		Superintended clipping of horses through 8th Corps Dipping Bath; inspected animals of 118 Inf Bde. & 50th M.V.S. routine office work.	
"	2nd		Superintended clipping of horses at 8th Corps Dipping Bath. inspected animals No 3 Scot; G.H.C. & 13/114. routine office work.	
"	3rd		Superintended clipping of horses at 8th Corps Dip. inspected animals at AVB Bty & 186 Bde R.F.A. general routine office work.	
"	4th		Superintended clipping of horses of 132 Fld Ambulance. inspected horses of 116 Inf Bde. routine office work.	
"	5th		Superintended clipping of horses at 8th Corps Dip; inspected horses of P/114 & P/186 Bdes R.F.A. +M.V.S. routine office work.	
"	6th		Superintended clipping of horses at 8th Corps Dip. inspected horses of 133 Fld Amb; 225 R.G.A. routine office work.	
"	7th		Superintended clipping of horses at 8th Corps Reif. inspected horses of No 1 Section D.A.C. & 50st M.V.S. routine office work.	
"	8th		Superintended clipping of horses at 8th Corps Dip; inspected horses of Divisional Train. general routine office work.	
"	9th		Superintended clipping of horses at 8th Corps Dip. inspected horses of 117 Infantry Bde. & routine office work.	
"	10th		Superintended clipping of horses at 8th Corps Dip. inspected 229 Co. R.E. & Mange cases, 13th Gloucesters. held conference with vety officers of 6/6 Bde; inspected horses of 116th	
"	11th		Superintended clipping of horses at R.F.A. +M.V.S. general routine office work.	
"	12th		Superintended clipping of horses at 8th Corps Dip. inspected 18 animals at M.V.S. Amb; 4/118 Inf Bde.	
"	13th		Superintended clipping of horses, inspected animals 134 Fld Amb; 4/118 Inf Bde.	
"	14th		Superintended clipping of horses at 8th Corps Dip; inspected horses of 116th Inf Bde. +Divisional Train. general routine office work.	

WAR DIARY
INTELLIGENCE SUMMARY
(Erase heading not required.)

Army Form C. 2118

ADVS. 39th Division

Place	Date	Hour	Summary of Events and Information	Remarks and references to Appendices
Poperinghe	Feb 1917 14th		Superintended dipping of horses of 8th Corps Dip; inspected horses No. 2 Sect type	
"	15th		Superintended dipping of horses at 8th Corps Dip; inspected horses of 119th Bde	
"	16th		transferred to 2nd R.Glos. R.F.A. general routine office work.	
"	17th		Superintended dipping of horses at 8th Corps Dip. inspected horses of B.H.Q.	
"	18th		Field conference with Vety. Officers at 8th Corps Dip. Inspected horses for	
"	19th		transfer to remounts, dipping of remounts, general routine office work.	
"	20th		Moved with Divisional Headquarters to Reninghelst.	
"			Handed over horse Dip 8th Corps to A.D.V.S. 55th Div.; inspected 53	
"	21st		animals in 50th M.V.S. prior to evacuation, routine office work.	
"	22nd		Inspected horses 111 Inf. Bde and 225 Coy R.E. general routine office	
"	23rd		work.	
"	24th		Inspected horses of 116 Inf. Bde & Divisional Train routine office work.	
"	25th		Inspected horses of "B" Bty. 186 Bde R.F.A. general routine office work.	
"	26th		Inspected horses A, B & C Btys 186 Bde R.F.A. for evacuation, routine office work.	
"	27th		Inspected horses of 174 Bde R.F.A. for evacuation & horses of both	
"	28th		Purchasing Board. general routine office work.	
"			Ordinary routine office work.	
"			Inspected horses of 50th M.V.S. & 116 Inf Bde general routine office work.	
"			Moved with Headquarters Division from Esquelbecq to Reninghelst.	
"			Confined to bed with severe chill.	

W.E.Barnes
Major A.V.C.
A.D.V.S. 39th Division

Army Form C. 2118

WAR DIARY or INTELLIGENCE SUMMARY

A.D.V.S. 39th Division   Vol 13

(Erase heading not required.)

Place	Date 1919	Hour	Summary of Events and Information	Remarks and references to Appendices
Remmingholst	Mar 1st		Visited M.V.S. and A.B Btys 174 Bde R.F.A. general routine office work.	
	2nd		Visited M.V.S. inspected animals of 13th Gloster. general routine office work	
	3rd		Visited MVS & inspected animals prior to evacuation. inspected animals of 234 Field Coy & 39 Sig. Coy. routine office work	
	4th		Visited "C" Bty 186 — inspected animals, inspected animals of 132 & 133 Fld Ambulances. general routine office work.	
	5th		Visited M.V.S. and inspected animals, inspected animals of 174 Bty 186 Bde R.F.A. general routine office work	
	6th		Visited M.V.S. inspected animals of 116 Inf Bde & 134 Field Ambulance. 225 Fld Coy R.E. general routine office work	
	7th		Visited M.V.S. met A.D.V.S. Army & 3 Feby 174 Bde & inspected animals. general routine office work	
	8th		Visited A.D. Btys 174 Bde R.F.A. general routine office work	
	9th		Held conference with Vety Officers visited M.V.S. routine office work	
	10th		Inspected 60 animals in M.V.S. prior to evacuation. inspected animals 13th Glosters. general routine office work.	
	11th		Inspected animals of Rus Hodar. general routine office work.	
	12th		Inspected animals of A,B Btys 186 Bde R.F.A. & 229 Fld Co R.E. general routine office work.	
	13th		Inspected animals of C,D Btys 186 Bde R.F.A. & 234 Fld Co R.E. general routine office work	
	14th		Inspected animals of 118 Inf. Bde. general routine office work	
	15th		Inspected remounts of No1 Coy Divisional Train, inspected animals of 132 Field Ambulance. general routine office work.	
	16th		Held conference with Vety Officers, inspected animals of 16th Sherwoods. inspected 16 animals in M.V.S. prior to evacuation. routine office work.	

Army Form C. 2118

WAR DIARY
or
INTELLIGENCE SUMMARY
(Erase heading not required.)

A.D.V.S. 39th Division.

Instructions regarding War Diaries and Intelligence Summaries are contained in F.S. Regs., Part II. and the Staff Manual respectively. Title Pages will be prepared in manuscript.

Place	Date	Hour	Summary of Events and Information	Remarks and references to Appendices
Remmughem	1917 March 18th		Superintended dipping of horses at 8th Corps Horse Exp. general routine office work.	
	19th		Inspected animals of 13th Gloucesters, A Bty 174 Bde R.F.A. & 39 Signal Coy. general routine office work.	
	20th		Inspected animals of 117 Inf Bde. general routine office work.	
	21st		Attended conference at Bailleul with D.D.V.S. 2nd Army, inspected animals of 225, 227 & 234 Coy R.E. general routine office work.	
	22nd		Held conference with Vety Officers of 186 Bde R.F.A. & A.S.C. B & D Bty 186 Bde R.F.A. & H routine office work.	
	23rd		Inspected animals 2 of Canadian Tunnelg Coy, M.V.S. & A Bty 186 Bde R.F.A. general routine office work.	
	24th		Superintended dipping of horses of 9th Corps Rip. Bouillaul; inspected 35 animals at M.V.S. prior to evacuation. routine office work.	
	25th		Inspected animals of 116 Inf Bde. general routine office work.	
	26th		Inspected animals of A, B & C Btys 174 Bde R.F.A. & 2nd Canadian Tunnelg Coy general routine office work.	
	27th		Inspected animals of 'B' Bty 188 Bde R.F.A. & D.H.Q. horses general routine office work.	
	28th		Inspected animals of Nos N°/B/143. Sect. 39 B.A.C. & 'B' Bty 186 Bde R.F.A. general routine office work.	
	29th		Inspected animals 13th Gloucesters, 1/6th Cheshires & 3/5th Alexandria Rgt. general routine office work.	
	30th		Inspected animals of 16th Rifle Bde & 17th K.R.R. general routine office work. Held conference with Vety Officers, visited M.V.S. general routine office work.	
	31st		Inspected animals of A, B & D Btys 186 Bde R.F.A. general routine office work.	

W. Buchanan
Col. A.V.C.
A.D.V.S. 39 Division.

WAR DIARY or INTELLIGENCE SUMMARY

Army Form C. 2118

(Erase heading not required.)

A.D.V.S. 39th Division

Vol 14

Place	Date	Hour	Summary of Events and Information	Remarks and references to Appendices
Reninghelst	April 1st 1917		Inspected animals of 39 Divisional Train, general routine office work.	
	2nd		Visited M.V.S., inspected animals of 132 & 133 Field Ambulances.	
	3rd		Inspected animals of "A" Bty 186 Bde R.F.A. also "A" Bty 174 Bde R.F.A. and No 2 Section B.F.C., routine office work.	
	4th		Inspected animals of 125th Siege Bty and whole of 174th Bde R.F.A.	
	5th		Inspected animals of Divisional Train & 14th Hants, routine office work.	
	6th		Inspected animals of M.V.S., & "B" Bty 174 Bde R.F.A. & Salvage Section.	
	7th		Inspected animals and "C" 186th Bde R.F.A., general routine office work.	
	8th		Inspected 14 animals at M.V.S. prior to evacuation. Visited VIII Corps stores Dep, No 1 Coy A.S.C. & 13th Gloster routine office work.	
	9th		Inspected animals of 132 Field Ambulance and visited M.V.S.	
	10th		Inspected animals 2nd Canadian Bnly Coy, 1st Canadian Rly Troop, & 501 Section D.A.C. and "D" 174 Bde R.F.A. arranged move of M.V.S. to Dickebusch. routine office work.	
	11th		Visited 118th Inf Bde and M.V.S. new site, general routine office work & 1/1 Cheshire Regt.	
	12th		Inspected animals of 227 Field Coy R.E. and 50th M.V.S., & 13th Gloster general routine office work.	
	13th		Inspected animals of 174 Bde R.F.A. "D" 186 Bde R.F.A. and MMP animals at R.H.Q. general routine office work.	
	14th		Inspected animals of 119 Inf Bde, & No 2 Coy ASC. & 132 Field Ambulance general routine office work.	
	15th		Visited M.V.S. and inspected 20 animals prior to evacuation, inspected animals of No 3 Section D.A.C. general routine office work.	

Army Form C. 2118

WAR DIARY
or
INTELLIGENCE SUMMARY
(Erase heading not required.)

A.D.V.S. 39th Division

Instructions regarding War Diaries and Intelligence Summaries are contained in F. S. Regs., Part II. and the Staff Manual respectively. Title Pages will be prepared in manuscript.

Place	Date 1917	Hour	Summary of Events and Information	Remarks and references to Appendices
Ronningfelot	Apl 16th		Inspected animals of 234 & 225 Coys R.E. and 116 Inf. Bde. general routine office work.	
	17th		Inspected animals of D.H.Q. and 11th & 13th Sussex Regt. and 3rd & 4th Coy A.S.C. general routine office work.	
	18th		Visited and inspected 174th Bde. R.F.A. and M.V.S. & 118th Inf. Bde. general routine office work.	
	19th		Inspected animals of Nos 1 & 2 Coys A.S.C. & 133 & 134 Field Amb: general routine office work.	
	20th		Visited M.V.S. & inspected 29 animals prior to evacuation. general routine office work.	
	21st		Visited 186th Bde. & inspected animals visited 234 & 60 R.E. general routine office work.	
	22nd		Visited 13 Geaters and ½ Comm and inspected animals general routine office work.	
	23rd		Inspected animals of 174th Bde. R.F.A. and M.V.S. general routine office work.	
	24th		Visited & inspected animals 298 Bde R.F.A. and 224 & 60 R.E. general routine office work.	
	25th		Inspected animals of D.H.Q. and Divisional Train. general routine office work.	
	26th		Visited VIII Corps Store Dip re dipping of animals 116 M.G. Coy. general routine office work.	
	27th		Inspected animals of 13 Geaters & 234 Coy R.E. general routine office work.	
	28th		Visited M.V.S. and inspected animals prior to evacuation. routine office work.	
	29th		Visited 117th Inf Bde. and Divisional Train + 132 Field Ambulance. general routine office work.	
	30th		Moved with Divisional Headquarters to "D" Camp. A 30 c 2 2. routine office work.	

Vol 15 Army Form C. 2118.

A.D.V.S. 39 Div

WAR DIARY
INTELLIGENCE SUMMARY
(Erase heading not required.)

Place	Date	Hour	Summary of Events and Information	Remarks and references to Appendices
Borden Camps	MAY 1915			
	1st		Visited and inspected animals of Bombs & Black Watch Regts. general routine office work.	
	2nd		Inspected animals Divisional Train, 298 Bde A.F.A. and 186 Bde R.F.A.	
	3rd		Inspected animals of 50th M.V.S. routine office work.	
	4th		Inspected animals of 225 Coy R.E. & Bk Watch Regt., routine office work	
	5th		Visited 227 Coy & 234 Coy R.E. general routine office work.	
			Inspected animals of 13 Gloster Regt. & 132 Field Ambulance general routine office work.	
	6th		Inspected fourteen animals at 50th M.V.S. prior to evacuation; inspected animals of 194 Bde R.F.A. general routine office work.	
	7th		Inspected animals of 133 & 134 Field Ambulances, routine office work.	
	8th		Inspected animals of Cheshire, Bombs & Herts Regts & № 3 Coy A.S.C. general routine office work.	
	9th		Inspected animals of SV.1 Section B.A.C. & A 298 A.F.A. Bde general routine office work.	
	10th		Inspected animals of Nos 1 & 2 Coys A.S.C. routine office work.	
	11th		Inspected D.H.Q animals & 13 Glosters & 39 hq Coy animals general routine office work.	

Army Form C. 2118.

WAR DIARY
or
INTELLIGENCE SUMMARY.
(Erase heading not required.)

A.D.V.S. 39 Division.

Instructions regarding War Diaries and Intelligence Summaries are contained in F. S. Regs., Part II. and the Staff Manual respectively. Title pages will be prepared in manuscript.

Place	Date	Hour	Summary of Events and Information	Remarks and references to Appendices
Borden Camp	May 1917			
	12th		Inspected animals of 118th Inf Bde, general routine office work.	
	13th		Visited 174 Bde R.F.A. & inspected animals, routine office work.	
	14th		Inspected animals of No 1 & 3 Sections 39 DAC routine office work.	
	15th		Inspected animals of 119th Inf Bde, general routine office work.	
	16th		Visited 174 Bde, R.F.A., 50th M.V.S. & 116 Inf Bde, routine office work.	
	17th		Inspected animals of 132, 133 & 134 Field Ambs, routine office work.	
	18th		Held conference with Veterinary Officers, routine office work.	
	19th		Inspected animals of 118 Inf Bde, - 13 Gloster Regt. general routine office work.	
	20th		Visited 50th M.V.S. inspected 11 animals prior to evacuation. general. routine office work.	
	21st		Inspected animals of 298th Bde A.F.A. general routine office work.	
	22nd		Inspected animals of 117th Infantry Brigades, general routine office work.	
	23rd		Acted as a judge at 39th Signal Company's sports, general routine office work.	

Army Form C. 2118.

WAR DIARY
or
INTELLIGENCE SUMMARY.
(Erase heading not required.)

A.D.Y.S. 39 Div.

Instructions regarding War Diaries and Intelligence Summaries are contained in F. S. Regs., Part II. and the Staff Manual respectively. Title pages will be prepared in manuscript.

Place	Date	Hour	Summary of Events and Information	Remarks and references to Appendices
Borden Camp	MAY 1917			
	24th		Visited 39th D.A.C. & 13 Gloster Regt. general routine office work.	
	25th		Held conference with Veterinary Officers routine office work.	
	26th		Arranged for 250 animals to be put through 8th Corps Horse Dip. general routine office work.	
	27th		Visited & inspected animals of A.B. & G Batteries 186 Bde R.F.A. general routine office work.	
	28th		Inspected animals of four companies 39 Divisional Train, & 132 Field Ambulance; general routine office work.	
	29th		Inspected animals of 133 & 134 Field Ambulance general routine office work.	
	30th		Inspected animals of 116 Inf Bde general routine office work.	
	31st		Inspected new site for 50th M.V.S. and arranged for moving of same. general routine office work.	

W E Barnes
Major AVC
ADVS 39 Div

WAR DIARY

INTELLIGENCE SUMMARY. D.A.D.V.S. 39th Division

Army Form C. 2118.

Vol 16

Place	Date	Hour	Summary of Events and Information	Remarks and references to Appendices
Border Camp.	June 1919			
	1st		Visited M.V.S; inspected animals of Nos 1 & 2 Sections 39th R.A.E; 39th Sig Coy; and A Bty 186th Bde R.F.A. general routine office work.	
	2nd		Inspected animals 19th K R R C, 16th R Rde, & 16th Notts Derbys. Visited M.V.S. general routine office work.	
	3rd		Inspected animals of 50th M.V.S, 11th & 12th Sussex. general routine office work.	
	4th		Acted as a judge at Divisional Train Horse Show. routine office work.	
	5th		Visited M.V.S. and 132nd 133rd Field Ambulances; visited Divisional Schools; general routine office work.	
	6th		Acted as a judge at Horse Show. 118th Infy. Bde. routine office work.	
	7th		Inspected animals of 11th, 12th & 13th Sussex; inspected animals at Divisional Schools. general routine office work.	
	8th		Inspected animals of 31st & 132nd Labour Companies, 2nd Bn Canadian Rly Troops and 39th Signal Coy; general routine office work.	
	9th		Inspected animals of M.V.S; held conference with Veterinary Officers. inspected 13 animals at M.V.S prior to evacuation. routine office work.	
	10th		Visited 39th Divisional Schools & arranged for evacuation of two horses. general routine office work.	

Army Form C. 2118.

WAR DIARY

INTELLIGENCE SUMMARY

(Erase heading not required.)

Instructions regarding War Diaries and Intelligence Summaries are contained in F. S. Regs., Part II. and the Staff Manual respectively. Title pages will be prepared in manuscript.

Place	Date June 1919.	Hour	Summary of Events and Information	Remarks and references to Appendices
Borden Camp.	11th		Inspected animals of 134th Field Ambulance, and 14th Hoants. general routine office work.	
	12th		Visited 116th Infantry Brigade, and re-classified all the animals. general routine office work.	
	13th		Inspected animals of M.V.S. and 39th D.A.C. general routine office work.	
	14th		Inspected animals of 225th, 227th Companies R.E., & 13th Gloucrs. general routine office work.	
	15th		Held conference with Veterinary Officers. inspected animals of 134th Field Ambulance, general routine office work.	
	16th		Visited 50th M.V.S. and inspected 19 animals prior to evacuations. general routine office work.	
	17th		Inspected animals of 7th Bde. A.F.A. general routine office work.	
	18th		Visited all units in training area. routine office work.	
	19th		Visited 50th M.V.S, 116th Inf Bde & 39th D.A.C. routine office work.	
	20th		Attended conference with D.V.S. general routine office work.	
	21st		Inspected animals of A, B & C Btys 186th Bde R.F.A. general routine office work.	

Army Form C. 2118.

WAR DIARY
or
INTELLIGENCE SUMMARY.
(Erase heading not required.)

Place	Date	Hour	Summary of Events and Information	Remarks and references to Appendices
Borden Camp.	June 1917			
	22nd		Held conference with Veterinary Officers, general routine office work.	
	23rd		Inspected animals of the 174th Bde R.F.A. general routine office work.	
	24th		Visited 50th M.V.S. inspected animals of 114th Inf Bde. routine office work.	
	25th		Inspected animals of the 39th B.A.C. general routine office work.	
	26th		Visited 50th M.V.S. and inspected 25 animals prior to evacuation. general routine office work	
	27th		Visited 118th Inf Bde and arranged for evacuation of 3 animals general routine office work.	
	28th		Visited & inspected 18th Corps Horse Dip. routine office work.	
	29th		Held conference with Veterinary Officers. Visited 18th Corps Horse Dip. Visited 192nd Labour company; general routine Office work.	
	30th		Visited 18th Corps Horse Dip. morning & evening; general routine office work.	

W.G.Barnes
Major A.V.C.
A.D.V.S. 39th Division

WAR DIARY or INTELLIGENCE SUMMARY

Army Form C. 2118.

D.A.D.V.S. 39 Division

Reference Appx one

Place	Date	Hour	Summary of Events and Information	Remarks
Borden Camp.	July 1st 1917		Visited 18th Corps Horse Dep. Conference with A.D.V.S. 18th Corps.	
"	2nd		Visited, & inspected 39 animals of 50 M.V.S. prior to evacuation. Visited Dep. general routine office work.	
"	3rd		Moved with Headqrs from Borden Camp to Quarry Camp (A.30. central Sheet 28 N.W.) routine office work.	
Quarry Camp.	4th		Inspected animals 118 Inf. Bde. Visited Horse Dep. routine office work.	
"	5th		Superintended dipping of animals at Horse Dep. routine office work.	
"	6th		Held conference with Vety Officers. Visited Horse Dep.	
"	7th		Attended conference with A.D.V.S. 18th Corps. general routine office work.	
"	8th		Major W.J.Barnes proceeded on leave. Capt. W.A. Buchanan A.V.C. took over duties.	
"	9th		Visited 18th Corps Horse Dep. inspected animals of R.M.C. routine office work	
"	10th		Visited M.V.S. & 18th Corps Horse Dep. inspected animals of 118 I.F. Bde.	
"	11th		Visited Horse Dep. inspected animals of 132,133, & 134 Fd. Ambs. routine office work.	
"	12th		Inspected animals of 2/15 Co RE, 34th A.F.A. Bde. Visited Dep. routine office work.	
"	13th		Held conference with Vety Officers. Visited Dep. general routine office work.	
"	14th		Attended conference with A.D.V.S. 18th Corps. Visited 175 A.F.A. Bde. routine office work	

WAR DIARY
or
INTELLIGENCE SUMMARY.
(Erase heading not required.)

Army Form C. 2118.

BA DVS. 39 Division

Place	Date	Hour	Summary of Events and Information	Remarks and references to Appendices
Quarry Camp.	July 1917			
	15th		Visited 18th Corps Horse Dip. inspected animals of 194 Bde R.F.A. general routine office work.	
	16th		Inspected animals of 186 Bde R.F.A. & 234 Fd Co R.E. general office work. visited Dip	
ˮ	17th		Visited M.V.S. & Dip. inspected animals of 240 Bde R.F.A. general routine office work.	
ˮ	18th		Inspected animals of HSt BA.C, 494th Fd Co R.E. general routine office work.	
ˮ	19th		Visited Dip & M.Y.S. inspected animals 241 Bde R.F.A. general routine office work.	
ˮ	20th		Held conference with Vety Officers inspected 36 animals at M.V.S. prior to evacuation.	
ˮ	21st		Handed over duties to Major Barnes AVC. returned off leave. attended Corps Conf	
ˮ	22nd		Inspected animals of 39 B.R.C. visited Horse Dip. routine office work.	
ˮ	23rd		Visited Horse Dip. & M.V.S. inspected animals 227 Co R.E. general routine office work.	
ˮ	24th		Inspected animals 186 Bde R.F.A & 132, 133, 134, Fd Ambs. Visited Horse Dip routine office work.	
ˮ	25th		Inspected animals of 118 & 116 Inf Bdes. visited MVS & Dip routine office work.	
ˮ	26th		attended airfience JHQ 39 Div	
ˮ	26th		Visited & inspected 39 animals at SOM.V.S. prior to evacuation. routine office work.	
ˮ	27th		Held conference with V.O's inspected 13 Gluster. routine office work.	
ˮ	28th		Attended conference with A. DVS. 18th Corps. general routine office work.	
ˮ	29th		Visited M.V.S. arranged site for New Vety Dressing Station & personnel.	
ˮ	30th		Visited 18th Corps Horse Dip. M.V.S. & Dressing Station. routine office work.	
ˮ	31st		Visited M.V.S. Dip & Dressing Station. general routine office work.	

WAR DIARY
INTELLIGENCE SUMMARY
(Erase heading not required.)

D.A.D.V.S. CENTRE 18 DIVISION

D.A.D.V.S. 39th Division

Place	Date 1917	Hour	Summary of Events and Information	Remarks and references to Appendices
Query Camp.	Aug: 1st		Visited 18th Corps Horse Disp. & A.V.D.S. arranged for advance of same. general routine office work.	
"	2nd		Inspected animals of 174 Bde R.F.A. & visited Ado Vety Dressing Station. general routine office work.	
"	3rd		Conference with Vety Officers. Inspected 36 animals at M.V.S. prior to evacuation. general routine office work.	
"	4th		Attended conference with A.D.V.S. Corps. general routine office work.	
"	5th		Inspected 32 animals at 50th M.V.S. general routine office work.	
"	6th		general routine office work. visited 50th M.V.S.	
"	7th		Moved with Divisional Headqrs from Query Camp to METEREN	
METEREN	8th		Arranged move of 50th M.V.S. from A.21.c.9-7(2s) to R.21.a.5-3(7) Inspected animals of R.H.Q. M.V.S. & Sig. Coy. routine office work.	
"	9th		Inspected animals of 227 & 225 Coys R.E. 132 Fld Amb. routine office work.	
"	10th		Attended Conference with A.D.V.S. Corps. inspected animals 116 Inf Bde. routine office work.	
"	11th		Inspected animals of 118 & 117 Inf Bdes. 13 Gloster. 133rd Fld Amb general routine office work.	
"	12th			
"	13th		Inspected animals of Nos 2, 3, 4 Coys 39th Div. Pio. Train. 228 M.G. Coy. general routine office work.	

WAR DIARY or INTELLIGENCE SUMMARY

Army Form C.2118.

DA DVS. 39 Division

Place	Date	Hour	Summary of Events and Information	Remarks and references to Appendices
METEREN	Aug. 1917 14th		arranged move of 50 MVS from R.21.a.5.3 (27) to LA CLYTTE.	
			Inspected animals of 134 Fd Amb & 116 Inf Bde. general routine office work.	
	15th		Moved with Divisional Headqrs from METEREN to WESTOUTRE.	
	16th		Inspected animals of M.V.S. 117th Inf Bde. general routine office work.	
	17th		Inspected 83 animals of M.V.S. prior to evacuation. Conf with Vety Officer	
	18th		Conference of ADVS & Corps. Inspected animals No 2 & 3 Coy ASC.	
	19th		Inspected animals 132 Fd Amb & 133 Fd Amb general routine office work.	
	20th		Inspected animals of 116 & 118 Inf Bdes. general routine office work	
	21st		Inspected animals of 13 Ulsters. M.V.S. + 225, 227, 234 Coys R.E. routine office work	
	22nd		Visited ADVS. Corps. + M.V.S. + 228 M.G. Coy. general routine office work.	
	23rd		Inspected animals of 174th Bde + D.A.C. general routine office work.	
	24th		Vety Officers Conference. inspected animals 186 Bde RFA routine office work	
	25th		Conference with ADVS Corps. general routine office work.	
	26th		Inspected animals 117 & 118 Inf Bdes. routine office work.	
	27th		Inspected 48 animals of M.V.S. prior to evacuation, routine office work.	
	28th		Visited ADVS Corps. inspected animals 227 Coy R.E. routine office work.	
	29th		Inspected animals 116 Inf Bde. 234 Coy R.E. general routine office work.	
	30th		ADVS being inspected animals of 186 & 174 Bdes R.F.A. routine office work.	
	31st		animals of 174th Bde R.F.A. inspected by Shoemaster Corps. routine office work. conference with Vety Officers	

E.A.Barnes

WAR DIARY
INTELLIGENCE SUMMARY

D.A.D.V.S. 39 Division

Place	Date 1917	Hour	Summary of Events and Information	Remarks
Westoutre	1st		Attended conference A.D.V.S. 10 Corps. general routine office work.	
"	2nd		Took over duties of A.D.V.S. 10 Corps, during his absence on leave.	
"	3rd		Inspected animals of 116th Infy Bde & 228 M.G. Coy. routine office work.	
"	4th		Visited 50th M.V.S. + 225, 227 Fd. Coy. R.E. general routine office work.	
"	5th		Inspected animals of 117 Infy Bde, & visited 174 Bde R.F.A. routine office work.	
"	6th		Inspected animals of Corps Units. & 137 Gleaters. general routine office work.	
"	7th		Held conference with D.Os. general routine office work.	
"	8th		Conference at Corps; inspected 118th Infy Bde animals prior to evacuation.	
"	9th		Visited 50th M.V.S. + inspected 32 animals prior to evacuation.	
"	10th		Inspected animals of 186 Bde R.F.A. & 234 Coy R/E. general routine office work.	
"	11th		Inspected animals of 132, 133, Fd Amb. general routine office work.	
"	12th		Office moved from Westoutre to Rezon Camp. routine office work.	
Rezon Camp	13th		Inspected animals of 134 Fd Amb. & No 1 Coy. Div. Train. routine office work.	
"	14th		Held conference with V.Os. inspected animals No 2 Coy A.S.C.	
"	15th		Conference at Corps. inspected animals of No 4 + No 3 Coy A.S.C.	
"	16th		Gave up duties of A.D.V.S. Corps. inspected 30 animals at M.V.S. prior to evacuation general routine office work.	

Army Form C. 2118.

WAR DIARY
or
INTELLIGENCE SUMMARY.   D.A.D.V.S. 39th Division
(Erase heading not required.)

Instructions regarding War Diaries and Intelligence Summaries are contained in F. S. Regs., Part II. and the Staff Manual respectively. Title pages will be prepared in manuscript.

Place	Date	Hour	Summary of Events and Information	Remarks and references to Appendices
Bn Camp	Sept 17th		Inspected animals of 117 Inf Bde, & 13 Bn Gloster routine office work.	
"	18th		Inspected animals of 186 Bde & R.A.C. general routine office work.	
"	19th		Inspected animals 228 M.G. Coy, 227 Fd Coy R.E. routine office work.	
"	20th		Inspected animals of Div train & 13th Fd Amb general routine office work.	
"	21st		Held conference with V.Os. visited 174 Bde R.F.A. routine office work.	
"	22nd		Attended conference of ADVS Corps. general routine office work.	
"	23rd		Office moved from Be Zon Camp to Zevecoten. routine office work.	
Zevecoten	24th		Inspected 43 animals at M.V.S. prior to evacuation. routine office work.	
"	25th		Inspected animals 116 Inf Bde, – 234 Coy R.E. general routine office work.	
"	26th		Visited M.V.S. inspected animals of 134th, 133 Fd Amb routine office work.	
"	27th		Visited 39th DAC & 186 Bde R.F.A. inspected 118 Inf Bde animals	
"	28th		Office moved from Zevecoten to St Jans Cappel. conference with V.Os.	
St Jans Cappel	29th		Corps conference. ADVS. visited 116 Inf Bde general routine office work.	
"	30th		Visited M.V.S. 186 & 174 Bde. No 4 Coy ASC general routine office work.	

Major DADVS 39th Division

WAR DIARY
or
INTELLIGENCE SUMMARY.
(Erase heading not required.)

Army Form C. 2118.

D.A.D.V.S. 39th Division

WA 20

Place	Date	Hour	Summary of Events and Information	Remarks and references to Appendices
Caestre / ST JANS CAPPEL	1917 1st		Visited 50th M.V.S., 225 and 227 Field Coy. R.E's. general routine office work.	
	2nd		Visited 50 M.V.S. and 116 Infantry Bde: routine office work.	
	3rd		Visited 50 M.V.S. routine office work. Capt Skelton granted leave. Major Barnes acting O.C. M.V.S.	
	4th		Visited 50 M.V.S. and 117th Infantry Bde.	
	5th		Attended V.O's conference and visited 50 M.V.S., general routine office work.	
	6th		Inspected 23 animals at 50 M.V.S. prior to evacuation. Attended Corps conference, and visited 50 Coy. A.S.C.	
	7th		Inspected animals of 13th Gloucesters and H/s Black Watch, and visited 50 M.V.S.	
	8th		Inspected animals of 117 Infantry Bde, & 39 Div. Train, also visited 50 M.V.S. routine office work.	
	9th		Visited 50 M.V.S. 117 Infantry Bde. 186 Bde and 174 Bde of Artillery and No 1 Coy. A.S.C.	
	10th		Inspected animals of 225 Field Coy. R.E. and No 4. Coy: A.S.C. and visited 50 M.V.S.	
	11th		Visited 50 M.V.S. 174 & 176 Bdes of Artillery and 228 Field Coy: R.E. general routine office work.	
	12th		Held conference with V.O's, visited 50 M.V.S. and inspected animals of 116th Inf. Bde. and 13th Gloucesters.	
	13th		Visited 50 M.V.S. q inspected 17 animals prior to evacuation. Attended conference at Corps.	
	14th		Visited 50 M.V.S. and inspected animals of the 116th Inf. Bde. and 174 Bde R.F.A. routine office work.	
	15th		Visited 50 M.V.S. general routine office work.	
	16th		Office moved from ST JANS CAPPEL to DE ZON CAMP (M12c5-1) general routine office work.	

E.J. Barnes Major
D.A.D.V.S. 39th Division

WAR DIARY
or
INTELLIGENCE SUMMARY.
(Erase heading not required.)

Army Form C. 2118.

D.A.D.V.S. 39th Division

Place	Date	Hour	Summary of Events and Information	Remarks and references to Appendices
October 1917				
DE ZON CAMP.	17th		Visited 50th M.V.S. General office work.	
	18th		Visited 50th M.V.S. General office work.	
	20th		Visited 50th M.V.S. Routine office work.	
	21st		Inspected animals of 39 Artillery at STRAZEELE. Capt Skelton started for leave.	
	22nd		Inspected animals of 116 & 118 Infantry Bde's. routine office work.	
	23rd		Inspected animals of 39th D.A.C. routine office work.	
	24th		Visited 50th M.V.S. and inspected animals of 117 Inf. Bde.	
	25th		Inspected animals of the 39 Artillery at STRAZEELE, general routine office work.	
	26th		Visited 50th M.V.S. general routine office work.	
	27th		Attended conference at Corps. Visited 50th M.V.S.	
	28th		Went to WESTOUTRE to arrange central clothing stable. routine office work.	
	29th		Visited 50th M.V.S. general routine office work.	
	30th		Visited A.D.V.S. Corps. general routine office work.	
	31st		Conference A.D.V.S. visited 50th M.V.S. and clothing stable. general routine office work.	

W.E. Barnes Major
D.A.D.V.S. 39th Divn

Army Form C. 2118.

WAR DIARY
or
INTELLIGENCE SUMMARY.
(Erase heading not required.)

D.A.D.V.S. 80TH DIVISION

B.A. D.V.S. 39th Division

Vol 21

Instructions regarding War Diaries and Intelligence Summaries are contained in F. S. Regs., Part II. and the Staff Manual respectively. Title pages will be prepared in manuscript.

Place	Date	Hour	Summary of Events and Information	Remarks and references to Appendices
Div.Hqrs.Camp.	Nov 1st 1917		Inspected 49 animals at M.V.S. prior to evacuation. Visited Clipping Stable. routine office work.	
"	2nd		Inspected animals of 118 Inf Bde. & 228 M.G. Coy. visited Clipping Stable & M.V.S. routine office work	
"	3rd		Attended conference at A.D.V.S. Corps. visited M.V.S. general routine office work.	
"	4th		Visited Clipping Shed and M.V.S. inspected animals of 116 Inf Bde routine office work.	
"	5th		Visited M.V.S. inspected animals of Div Train. visited Clipping Shed. "	
"	6th		Visited M.V.S. inspected 20 animals prior to evacuation. general routine office work.	
"	7th		Inspected animals of 186 Bde R.F.A. & 132 Fd Amb. visited Clipping Shed.	
"	8th		Visited M.V.S. & inspected 69 animals prior to evacuation. visited Clipping Shed routine office work.	
"	9th		Held conference with Vety Officers. visited Clipping Shed. & M.V.S. routine office work.	
"	10th		Attended conference with A.D.V.S. Corps. visited M.V.S. Clipping shed & 133 & 134 Fd Ambs.	
"	11th		Inspected animals of B.H.Q. & 13 Yorks. visited Clipping Shed. routine office work.	
"	12th		Inspected animals of B.H.Q. & Signal Coy. visited M.V.S. & Clipping Shed. routine office work.	
"	13th		Inspected animals of 114 Bde R.F.A. visited Div Train. & M.V.S. general routine office work.	
"	14th		Visited Clipping Shed. & M.V.S. inspected animals 225 & 234 R.Ebo routine office work.	
"	15th		Visited M.V.S. & inspected 39 animals prior to evacuation. inspected animals of 227.60 R.E.	
"	16th		Moved with B.H.Q. to Westoutre; held conference with Vety Officers	

Army Form C. 2118.

D.A.D.V.S.
30TH DIVISION.

WAR DIARY
or
INTELLIGENCE SUMMARY.

(Erase heading not required.)

D.A.D.V.S. 39th Division

Instructions regarding War Diaries and Intelligence Summaries are contained in F. S. Regs., Part II and the Staff Manual respectively. Title pages will be prepared in manuscript.

Place	Date Nov 1917	Hour	Summary of Events and Information	Remarks and references to Appendices
Westoutre	17th		Attended conference with A.D.V.S. Corps. inspected animals of 117th Inf. Bde.	
"	18th		Clipping Shed broken up. arranged for disposal of men machines &c.	
"	19th		Visited M.V.S. handed over clipping shed to Chev. Comdt. routine office work.	
"	20th		Inspected animals of 186 Bde R.F.A., general routine office work.	
"	21st		Major Barnes R.Y.C. proceeded on leave, Capt Strallson A.V.C. d/c M.V.S. performing duties.	
"	22nd		Inspected 93 animals at M.V.S. prior to evacuation routine office work.	
"	23rd		Held conference with V.O's. inspected animals of 117th Inf Bde.	
"	24th		Attended conference with A.D.V.S. Corps. general routine office work.	
"	25th		Inspected animals of 116th & 118th Inf Bdes. general routine office work.	
"	26th		Moved M.V.S. from Reninge camp to Watou.	
"	27th		Moved with R.Q.Hd. from Westoutre to Steenwoorde. general routine office work.	
"	28th		Visited A.D.V.S. 8th Corps. at Corps H.Q. general routine office work.	
"	29th		Inspected 94 animals at M.V.S. prior to evacuation. routine office work.	
"	30th		Held conference with V.O's. inspected animals R.Q.H.Q. routine office work.	

Chilson
Capt.
for D.A.D.V.S. 39th Division.

Army Form C. 2118.

WAR DIARY
or
INTELLIGENCE SUMMARY.
(Erase heading not required.)

DA DVS. 39th Division

Place	Date 1917	Hour	Summary of Events and Information	Remarks and references to Appendices
Steenwoorde	December 1st		Visited 50th M.V.S. and attended conference with A.D.V.S. Corps.	
"	2nd		Visited DHQ. Inspected animals. Inspected animals No 4 Coy Train.	
"	3rd		Visited 116 Inf Bde & inspected animals – general routine office work.	
"	4th		Inspected animals 118th Inf Bde. General routine office work.	
"	5th		Inspected animals of 132nd Field Ambulance. & No 2 & 3 Coys A.S.C.	
"	6th		Inspected 28 animals at 50th M.V.S. prior to evacuation general office work.	
"	7th		Held conference with Vet. Offrs. Inspected animals 119 Inf Bde.	
"	8th		Attended conference with A.D.V.S. Corps. – inspected animals 174 & 186 Bdes R.F.A.	
"	9th		Moved M.Y.S. from Watones to Nielles Les Blecquin.	
"	10th		Moved office with DHQ from Steenwoorde to Nielles-Leg-Blecquin.	
Nielles Leg Blecquin.	11th		Arranged Billet for M.V.S. at Nielles Leg. Blecquin. routine office work	
"	12th		Inspected, at 50th M.V.S. 9 animals prior to evacuation.	
"	13th		Visited A.D.V.S. Corps. general routine office work.	
"	14th		Inspected animals 116 & Inf Bde. general routine office work.	
"	15th		Inspected animals of 50th M.V.S. & 39th Signal Coy.	
"	16th		Inspected animals of Divisional Headquarters. general routine office work.	

2353 Wt. W2514/1454 700,000 5/15 D.D.&L. A.D.S.S./Forms/C. 2118.

WAR DIARY or INTELLIGENCE SUMMARY

Army Form C. 2118.

BA DVS 39 Div

Place	Date Dec 1917	Hour	Summary of Events and Information	Remarks
Nielles les Blecquin	17th		Inspected animals of 228 M.&C.Coy. general routine office work.	
"	18th		Inspected animals No 2 Coy. ASC general routine office work.	
"	19th		Inspected animals 39th Sig Coy. general routine office work.	
"	20th		Inspected 6 animals at 50th M.V.S. prior to evacuation.	
"	21st		Arranged collection by flos, of 2 animals left at LICQUES.	
"	22nd		Inspected animals of 116 M.&C.Coy. & 14th Bn. Wards Regt. routine office work.	
"	23rd		Major W.F.Barnes RVC ret'd off leave, resumed duties BA DVS.	
"	24th		Inspected animals of 13 Sussex Regt. general routine office work.	
"	25th		General routine office work.	
"	26th		Inspected animals of 11th & 12th Btns Sussex Regt. routine office work.	
"	27th		Inspected animals at 50th M.V.S. 10 animals prior to evacuation routine office work.	
"	28th		Inspected animals of 39th Div. Signal Coy. routine office work.	
"	29th		General routine office work.	
"	30th		Moved with D.H.Q. from Nielles les Blecquin to Borden Camp.	
Borden Camp	31st		Inspected Billet for 50th M.V.S. general routine office work.	

Lt F Barnes Major

Army Form C. 2118.

WAR DIARY
or
INTELLIGENCE SUMMARY.
(Erase heading not required.)

D.A.D.V.S. 39th Div.

Vol 23

Place	Date	Hour	Summary of Events and Information	Remarks and references to Appendices
Borden Camp.	January 1918			
	1st		Arranged billet for 50th M.V.S. visited Odv Headqrs. general routine office work.	
"	2nd		Inspected animals of No 1 Coy A.S.C. & 174th Bde R.F.A. routine office work.	
"	3rd		Inspected animals of D.H.Q. visited 186 Bde R.F.A. routine office work.	
"	4th		Inspected remounts at Noorapeene. visited M.V.S. general routine office work.	
"	5th		Inspected animals of 116 Inf. Bde. 16th Notts R. & 50th M.V.S routine office work.	
"	6th		Inspected animals of 118 Inf. Bde. visited 50th M.V.S. routine office work.	
"	7th		Visited 50th M.V.S. inspected 26 animals prior to evacuation routine office work.	
"	8th		Inspected animals 228th M.G. Co, 13th Gloster & 118th M.G.Coy. routine office work	
"	9th		Inspected animals 225,226, & 234 Coys R.E. 116th M.G. Coy. general routine office work	
"	10th		Inspected animals 50th M.V.S. 16th Cheshires & 13th Sussex Rgt. routine office work.	
"	11th		Visited M.V.S. inspected animals 186 Bde R.F.A. routine office work.	
"	12th		Inspected animals of No 1 & 2. Sectn R.A.M.C. and 119 Inf. Bde. routine office work.	
"	13th		Held conference with Vety. Officers. inspected animals 11 Herts +H/5 Bde Water.	
"	14th		Inspected animals of 132 & 133 Fld Amb. general routine office work.	
"	15th		Inspected animals No 3 & 4 Coys. A.S.C. & 50th M.V.S. general routine office work.	
"	16th		Visited 186 Bde R.F.A. inspected animals 39 Sig Coy. routine office work.	

WAR DIARY
or
INTELLIGENCE SUMMARY.
(Erase heading not required.)

Army Form C. 2118.

A.D. Vs 39th Division

Place	Date Jany 1918	Hour	Summary of Events and Information	Remarks and references to Appendices
Borden Camp	17th		Visited 50th M.V.S. inspected 27 animals prior to evacuation routine office work.	
"	18th		Held conference with Sety Officers; visited 174th Bde R.F.A. routine office work.	
"	19th		Inspected animals of 116 Inf Bde R.F.A. general routine office work.	
"	20th		Inspected animals of 118 Inf Bde. 13 Gloster. "228 M.G.Cy. routine office work.	
"	21st		Visited 117 Inf Bde; inspected animals Div Train routine office work.	
"	22nd		Moved with D.H.Q. from Borden Camp to Barlhove Chateau Proven.	
Proven	23rd		Inspected animals 39 D.H.Q. & 39 Signal Coy. visited M.V.S. in new location.	
"	24th		Moved by lorries from Proven to Méricourt sur Somme.	
Méricourt sur Somme	25th		en route - arrived Méricourt sur Somme. 4 pm. routine office work.	
Méricourt sur Somme	26th		Arranged billets for 50th M.V.S. general routine office work.	
"	27th		Inspected animals 174th Bde R.F.A. & visited M.V.S. general routine office work.	
"	28th		Inspected animals 116 Inf Bde. no 3 Sect B.T.6. general routine office work.	
"	29th		Visited 50th M.V.S. no 2 Coy A.S.C. general routine office work.	
"	30th		Inspected animals. no 1 Coy A.S.C. & 50th M.V.S. 174th Bde R.F.A. routine office work.	
"	31st		Visited & inspected animals 186 Bde R.F.A. general routine office work.	

T.G. Barnes Major
A.D.Vrs 39 Division

WAR DIARY
INTELLIGENCE SUMMARY
(Erase heading not required.)

Army Form C. 2118.

DADVS 39th Div.

Place	Date	Hour	Summary of Events and Information	Remarks and references to Appendices
Imamount Sun Somme	February 1918. 1st		Visited 50th M.V.S. inspected animals of 194th Bde R.F.A routine office work.	
"	2nd		Moved with D.H.Q. from Maricourt sur Somme to Nurlu. routine office work.	
Nurlu	3rd		Attended office of ADVS Corps. inspected animals DAC routine office work.	
"	4th		Visited M.V.S. & inspected 41 animals prior to evacuation. routine office work.	
"	5th		Inspected animals 116 Inf Bde. & 134 Fd Amb. general routine office work.	
"	6th		Inspected animals of 186th Brigade R.F.A. visited M.V.S. routine office work.	
"	7th		Inspected animals of 118 Inf Bde. 225 & 234 Coys R.E. general routine office work.	
"	8th		Visited M.V.S. Inspected animals of 39 Sig Coy & 13th Border routine office work.	
"	9th		Held conference with V.O. of Division. Inspected animals of D.H.Q.	
"	10th		Attended conference at office of ADVS Corps. general routine office work.	
"	11th		Visited M.V.S. inspected 57 animals prior to evacuation. general routine office work.	
"	12th		Inspected animals 117 Inf Bde. & 132 +133 Fd Amb. general routine office	
"	13th		Inspected animals of 225 & 234 Coys R.E. visited attached Units	
"	14th		Visited M.V.S. inspected animals of 194 Bde R.F.A. general routine office work.	
"	15th		Visited 39th Div Train & inspected animals. general routine office work.	
"	16th		Held conference with Vety Officers general routine office work.	

Army Form C. 2118.

WAR DIARY
or
INTELLIGENCE SUMMARY.
(Erase heading not required.)

DA DVS 39 Div

Place	Date	Hour	Summary of Events and Information	Remarks and references to Appendices
Nienbu	February 1918 17th		Visited 116 Inf. Bde., attended to casualties caused by enemy bombing.	
"	18th		Visited M.V.S. inspected 47 animals prior to evacuation routine office work	
"	19th		Inspected remounts at No 1 Coy A.S.C. general routine office work.	
"	20th		Inspected animals of Nos 3 & 4 Coys A.S.C. visited 116 Inf. Bde. routine office work.	
"	21st		Inspected animals of 118 Inf. Bde. Gloucesters. routine office work.	
"	22nd		Visited office of ADVS 9 Corps & Corps H.Q. inspected animals of 117 Inf. Bde.	
"	23rd		Held conference with VOs of Division inspected animals of 186 Bde R.F.A.	
"	24th		Inspected animals of 228 M.G. Coy & 132 & 13 B Fld Amb, & 225 & 234 Fd Coys R.E.	
"	25th		Visited M.V.S. inspected 39 animals prior to evacuation. routine office work.	
"	26th		Inspected remounts & distributed same. general routine office work.	
"	27th		Visited 186 Bde R.F.A. & 116 Inf. Bde. visited 174 Bde R.F.A. 39 DAC.	
"	28th		Visited M.V.S. inspected animals of 284 Coy R.E. & Nos 1 & 2 Coys ASC routine office work.	

W.G. Barnes Major
DA DVS 39 Division

Army Form C. 2118.

WAR DIARY
or
INTELLIGENCE SUMMARY.
(Erase heading not required.)

Army No. 7 ADVS 39th Division

VI 25

Place	Date 1918	Hour	Summary of Events and Information	Remarks and references to Appendices
March	1st		Visited 50th M.V.S. & 186 Brigade R.F.A. general routine office work	
"	2nd		Inspected animals 39th Div. train. general routine office work.	
"	3rd		Inspected animals 39th Sig. Coy. general routine office work.	
"	4th		Visited 50 M.V.S. Inspected 12 animals prior to evacuation	
"	5th		Inspected animals of 174 Brigade R.F.A. general routine office work.	
"	6th		Inspected animals 39th D.A.C. & No 2 Coy Div. Train.	
"	7th		Visited Inspected animals 116 Inf Bde & 225 Coy R.E.	
"	8th		Held conference with Vety. Officers. general routine office work.	
"	9th		Visited ADVS 4th Corps at Corps Headqrs. general routine office work.	
"	10th		Inspected animals of 117th Inf. Bde. general routine office work.	
"	11th		Visited M.V.S. inspected 39 animals prior to evacuation.	
"	12th		Inspected animals 132, 133 Fd Amb. general routine office work.	
Hautallaines	13th		Moved with DHQ to Hautallaines. general routine office work.	
"	14th		Inspected 7 animals at M.V.S. prior to evacuation.	
"	15th		Inspected animals 118th Inf Bde. general routine office work	
"	16th		Inspected animals 134 Fd Amb. & 39th Sig Coy. routine office work.	

2353 Wt. W3544/1454 700,000 5/15 D.D.&L. A.D.S.S./Forms/C. 2118.

WAR DIARY
or
INTELLIGENCE SUMMARY.
(Erase heading not required.)

Army Form C. 2118.

BA DVS 39 Dn

Place	Date 1918	Hour	Summary of Events and Information	Remarks and references to Appendices
March Allonville	17th		Inspected animals of 186 Bde R.F.A. routine office work.	
"	18th		Visited M.V.S. Inspected 19 animals prior to evacuation.	
"	19th		Inspected animals 1914 Bde R.F.A. general routine office work.	
"	20th		Took over command of 50th M.V.S. vice Capt R.J. Stadden A.V.C on leave.	
"	21st		Office moved with D.H.Q. Holy Allaines to Foleny, thence to Fresne.	
"	22nd		" from Fresne to Chuignes	
"	23rd		" from Chuignes to Hamel.	
"	24th		" from Hamel to Demart sur la Luce.	
"	25th		" from Demart sur la Luce to Boves.	
"	26th		" from Boves to Guignemont.	
"	29th		" from Guignemont to Beeley St Leonards.	
"	30th		" from Beeley St Leonards to Crisemant	
"	31st		General routine office work.	

This formation landed in France 6/3/16

W.E. Barnes
BA DVS 39 Division

Army Form C. 2118.

14

WAR DIARY
or
INTELLIGENCE SUMMARY.
(Erase heading not required).

Instructions regarding War Diaries and Intelligence Summaries are contained in F. S. Regs., Part II. and the Staff Manual respectively. Title pages will be prepared in manuscript.

DA DVS 39 Div

Vol 26

Place	Date	Hour	Summary of Events and Information	Remarks and references to Appendices
April 1918	1st		Moved with M.V.S. from St Lucien to Guegnicourt.	
	2nd		" " " Guegnicourt to Fermy.	
	3rd		" " " Fermy to Andainville.	
Andainville	4th		Visited office of D.D.Q. general routine office work.	
"	5th		Visited office of D.D.Q. general routine office work.	
"	6th		Moved with M.V.S. from Andainville to Samaches.	
"	7th		Visited D.H.Q. at Samaches. Inspected animals of Div train	
"	8th		Office moved with D.H.Q. to Woincourt & entrained for St Omer.	
"	9th		" " " " to Zutkerque.	
"	10th		Capt Skelton returned off leave.	
Eperlecques	11th		Office moved with D.H.Q. from Zutkerque to Eperlecques.	
"	12th		Major Barnes resumed DADVS. work. general routine office work.	
"	13th		Inspected animals of Nos 2 & 3 Coys train. conference with Vet Officers	
"	14th		Inspected animals of 39 Sig Coy DHQ routine office work.	
"	15th		Visited inspected animals with surplus transport for American Div	
"	16th		Veterinary Officer in chief of 77th American Div visited office	

Army Form C. 2118.

WAR DIARY
or
INTELLIGENCE SUMMARY.
(Erase heading not required.)

ADMS 39 Div

Place	Date 1916	Hour	Summary of Events and Information	Remarks and references to Appendices
Etaples	17th		Inspected animals of M.V.S. routine office work.	
"	18th		Inspected animals of 50 M.V.S. prior to evacuation. Visited 77 Amer Div	
"	19th		Held conference with Vet Officers. general routine office work.	
"	20th		Inspected animals of surplus transport for Amer Div	
"	21st		Visited 50th M.V.S. & 77th American Division general routine office work	
"	22nd		Visited HQ. 116 Inf Bde. & 134th Fd Amb. general routine office work.	
"	23rd		Inspected animals No 293. Corps train general routine office work.	
"	24th		Visited M.V.S. inspected animals reequipment &c. routine office work.	
"	25th		Inspected animals 117th B. HQ. general routine office work.	
"	26th		Gave lecture on Vety work to Vet Officers 77 Amer Div. Visited No H.60 A.S.C.	
"	27th		Visited 77th American Division general routine office work.	
"	28th		Inspected animals surplus transport prior to being handed over to 77 Amer Div	
"	29th		Visited 118th Inf Bde HQ. general routine office work.	
"	30th		Visited Vet Hosp St Omer with Vety Officer 77th American Div	

This formation arrived in France 6/3/16
formed August 1915.

WAR DIARY

INTELLIGENCE SUMMARY

Army Form C. 2118.

D.A.D.V.S. 39th DIVISION.
No. VS.962
Date 1/6/1918.

DADVS. 39th Division

Vol 27

Place	Date 1918	Hour	Summary of Events and Information	Remarks and references to Appendices
Eqlléques	1st		Inspected animals of 116 Inf Bde details & 113 Glosters. routine office work.	
"	2nd		Visited 50th MVS. one animal evacuated. visited Div Vet 74th Amer Div	
"	3rd		Visited N°4 Coy ASC. inspected animals general routine office work.	
"	4th		Inspected animals 39th RMG. & rendered veterinary attention	
"	5th		Visited office of DVS. Army. Inspected animals of 119 Inf Bde details	
"	6th		Inspected animals 39th Sig Coy. & Div Headqs. general routine office work.	
"	7th		Visited office of Div Veterinarian 74th Amer Div. re arranging MVS instruction	
"	8th		Inspected animals of 225 Co RE, and 60pro troops attached.	
"	9th		Inspected animals of 118 Inf Bde general routine office work.	
"	10th		Inspected animals of 50 MVS. prior to evacuation general routine office work.	
"	11th		Visited American units in company Div Vet 74th Amer Div.	
"	12th		Visited office of ADVS Corps. Inspected animals N°4 60 A.S.C	
"	13th		Inspected 4 animals of 50th MVS. prior to evacuation routine office work.	
"	14th		Inspected animals of units prior to leaving Division routine office work.	
"	15th		Inspected 4 animals at 50th MVS. prior to evacuation routine office work.	
"	16th		Visited N°2 ADVS Base re medicines for Vet Officers units 74 Amer Division	

Confidential

Army Form C. 2118.

WAR DIARY
INTELLIGENCE SUMMARY.
(Erase heading not required.)

Instructions regarding War Diaries and Intelligence Summaries are contained in F. S. Regs., Part II. and the Staff Manual respectively. Title pages will be prepared in manuscript.

Place	Date 1916.	Hour	Summary of Events and Information	Remarks and references to Appendices
Eperlecques	17th		Inspected animals of Corps troops re general routine office work.	
"	18th		Major Welbourne AVC proceeded on 14 days leave. Capt R.I. Skelton AVC assumed duties temporarily. General routine office work.	
"	19th		Inspected 5 animals at 50th M.V.S. prior to evacuation routine office work.	
"	20th		Visited Div Vet 77th American Div. general routine office work.	
"	21st		77th M.V.S. now attached 50th M.V.S. for instruction	
"	22/19		Inspected animals 39th Dvl.Q + 39 Sig.Co general routine office work.	
"	23rd		Inspected animals of Army troops attached general routine office work.	
"	24th		Inspected animals No 4 Co A.S.C. general routine office work.	
"	25th		Evacuated 6 animals from 50th M.V.S.; visited Div.Vet 77 Amer Div.	
"	26th		Inspected animals 116 Inf Bde. general routine officework.	
"	27th		Instructed 77th Div in M.V.S. in general Vety work re general office work.	
"	28th		Inspected animals surplus, prior to being handed over to 30th Amer Div. Held conf with VOs 77th American Div.	
"	29th		Inspected surplus animals prior to being handed over to 30 Amer Div.	
"	30th		Visited Div Vet 77th American Div. general routine office work.	
"	31st		Visited Div Vet 77th Amer Div + arranged weekly returns re general routine officework.	

This formation was mobilized Aug 1915.

This formation arrived in France 6/3/1916.

[signature]
ADVS 39. Division

Army Form C. 2118.

WAR DIARY
or
INTELLIGENCE SUMMARY.
(Erase heading not required.)

ADMS 39th Div. Vol 28

Place	Date June 1918	Hour	Summary of Events and Information	Remarks and references to Appendices
Eperlecques	1st		Visited 30th & 74th American Div. Headqrs, general routine office work	
"	2nd		Visited No.3 Sect 19 Canadian Res Park. No.4 Coy ASC routine office work.	
"	3rd		— No.5 Sect 2nd Army Aux MT Co routine office work.	
"	4th		Major WJ Barnes assumed duties of ADMS 39 Division — " —	
"	5th		Inspected 28 animals at 50th M.Y.S. prior to evacuation — " —	
"	6th		Office moved from Eperlecques to Nielles-lez-Ardres. " —	
Nielles lez Ardres	7th		Inspected animals of 116th Inf Bde, details visited No.2 Bdn 119th Amer Bde.	
"	8th		Attended conference ADMS HQ 116th, visited 30th Amer BH.Q. re Mob Vet Sect.	
"	9th		Visited by DDVS. and proceeded with him round American units.	
"	10th		Proceeded to Calais by lorry to draw stores &c for 30th Amer Div	
"	11th		Proceeded by car & inspected all the Cadre Bdn's handed over by 34th Div	
"	12th		Inspected 4 animals at 50th M.Y.S. prior to evacuation routine office work.	
"	13th		Arranged Billet at Autingues for 50th M.Y.S. general routine office work.	
"	14th		Inspected animals being handed over to 30th Amer Div general — " —	
"	15th		Inspected animals 119th Inf Bde, attended handing over of animals to 30 Amer Div	
"	16th		Inspected animals of Cadre Bns 118th Inf Bn general routine office work.	

2353 Wt. W2544/1454 700,000 5/15 D. D. & L. A.D.S.S./Forms/C. 2118.

WAR DIARY
or
INTELLIGENCE SUMMARY.

Army Form C. 2118.

Place	Date	Hour	Summary of Events and Information	Remarks and references to Appendices
Nielles lez Ardres	June 1916			
	17th		Attending handing over of transport & horses &c. to 30th Amer. Div.	
,,	18th		Attended handing over of transport & horses &c. to 30th Amer Div routine office work.	
,,	19th		Attended handing over of transport & horses &c. to 30th Amer Div routine office work.	
,,	20th		Inspected 305 animals of M.Y.S. prior to evacn. attended handing over of horses to 30 Amer Div	
,,	21st		Inspected animals of Cadre Bn. handed over by 34th Div. visited 78th Amer Div	
,,	22nd		Visited 116th Inf. Bde H.Q. & called on Div Vet 78th Amer Div routine office work.	
,,	23rd		Visited 30th Amer Div accompanied by Div Veterinarian routine office work	
,,	24th		Arranged with 78th Div through 116th Bat Q. for lorry to go to Calais.	
,,	25th		Proceeded to No 2 B.V.Y.S. Calais for Vet Stores for 78th Amer Div routine office work.	
,,	26th		Inspected animals of Cadre Bn. 116th Bde & 78th Amer Div	
,,	27th		Inspected 14 animals of 50th M.V.S. prior to evacn. general routine office work.	
,,	28th		Visited Div Veterinarian 30th Amer Div inspected units of 30th Amer Div	
,,	29th		Called on Div Veterinarian 80th American Div. inspected units of Div.	
,,	30th		Inspected 11 horses at 50th M.V.S. prior to evacn. visited by DDVS 2Army	

This formation was mobilized Aug 1915.
arrived in France 6/3/1916.

W.G. Barnes
Major
D.A.D.V.S. 39 Division

Army Form C. 2118.

WAR DIARY
or
INTELLIGENCE SUMMARY
(Erase heading not required.)

D.A.D.V.S. 39th Division

VR 29

Place	Date 1918	Hour	Summary of Events and Information	Remarks and references to Appendices
Mullers les Anchers	1st July		Visited 50th M.V.S. Inspected animals 39th B.H.Q. Sig. Co. general routine office work.	
"	2nd		Visited Div. Vet. 30th Amer. Div., M.G. Units 30 Amer. Div., + 50th M.V.S. routine office work.	
"	3rd		Visited 117th Inf. Bde. reserve Battn. + 16th Div. Units general routine office work.	
"	4th		Visited 50th M.V.S. + Inspected 25 animals prior to evacuation. Visited 39th Div. train.	
"	5th		Visited D.H.Q. A.D.V.S. Corps. Inspected animals of 118th Inf. Bde. routine office work.	
"	6th		Visited 50th M.V.S., 116th Inf. Bde. + 78th American Div. units routine office work.	
"	7th		Inspected animals of 50th M.V.S. 39th Sig. Co. + Div. H.Q. general routine office work.	
"	8th		Proceeded to Mullers les Becquin to instruct Div. Vet 78th Amer. Div. in administrative work.	
"	9th		Inspected animals of 78th Amer. Div. and general routine office work.	
"	10th		Held conference with Vet Officers 78th Amer. Div. general routine office work.	
"	11th		Returned from Mullers les Becquin. Visited 50th M.V.S. Inspected 10 animals prior to evact.	
"	12th		Inspected animals of 2/20th + 2/24th London Regiments routine office work.	
"	13th		Visited D.H.Q. 450th M.V.S. proceeded to 119th Inf. Bde. Inspected animals 20th Amer. Div. M.G. Units general routine office work.	
"	14th		Visited A.D.V.S. Corps. Inspected animals No. 4 Coy A.S.C. routine office work.	
"	15th		Proceeded with A.D.V.S. Corps to 78th + 80th Amer. Div. + 119th Inf. Bde routine office work.	

Army Form C. 2118.

WAR DIARY
or
INTELLIGENCE SUMMARY.
(Erase heading not required.)

Instructions regarding War Diaries and Intelligence Summaries are contained in F.S. Regs., Part II and the Staff Manual respectively. Title pages will be prepared in manuscript.

Place	Date	Hour	Summary of Events and Information	Remarks and references to Appendices
Nullens / Andres	July 1915			
	16th		Visited 5th M.V.S. + 39th B.Vet. proceeded to 80th Amer. Div. M.G. units re case of anthrax.	
	17th		Proceeded with O.C. 39th Div. train to H.Q. 116th Inf. Bde. & Eadre Arms routine office work.	
	18th		Inspected 9 animals at M.V.S. prior to evacn. visited R.H.Q. routine office work.	
	19th		Inspected animals of 2/20th + 2/24th London Regts. + N° 4 Co A.S.C.	
	20th		Visited N°2 Base Report Vet. Stores arranged wallets scrimps for 134 F. Amb. conf with A.D.V.S. corps.	
	21st		Took over duties of A.D.V.S. corps. visited 13th Gloucester, 7th Cameron routine office work.	
	22nd		Visited office A.D.V.S. corps + 50th M.V.S. general routine office work.	
	24th		Visited No.2 B.Vets re veterinary medicines + 39th B.Vet.Q. general routine office work	
	25th		Visited M.V.S., N°s 2+3 Coys A.S.C., A.D.V.S. corps + 114th K.R.R.C. routine office work.	
	26th		Duties of A.D.V.S. 1st corps. visited M.V.S. + D.H.Q. routine office work.	
	27th		Duties of A.D.V.S. 1st corps. general routine office work.	
	28th		Major W.G. Barnes A.V.C. appts 2nd in command N°10 Vet. Hosp. Major H. Peele assumed duties D.A.D.V.S. 39th Div.	
	29th		Inspected R.H.Q. Police horses, visited 65th Bedn Regt. 50th M.V.S. + Div. Train H.Q. routine office work.	
	30th		Inspected animals 6th Bedn Regt. 114th R.H.Q. horses, 119th K.R.R.C. horses, 5th N. Staffs, 16th Sherw. Foresters + 11 Lokeshires	
	31st		Inspected animals of N° 4 Co A.S.C., 225 Co R.E., 13th Sussex Regt. 112th Fld Amb., 13th Gloster, N°s 2+3 Coys A.S.C., 118th Inf. R.H.Q. + 4th Bn Lincolns Regt. routine office work.	

This Summaries was motilized Aug. 1915
arrived in France 6/3/1916.

Haveyell
D.A.D.V.S. 39th Division

2353 Wt. W2544/1454 700,000 5/15 **D. D. & L.** A.D.S.S./Forms/C. 2118.

Army Form C. 2118.

WAR DIARY or INTELLIGENCE SUMMARY.
(Erase heading not required.)

D.A.D.V.S. 39th Division

Vol 30

Place	Date 1918	Hour	Summary of Events and Information	Remarks and references to Appendices
Nielles lez Ardres	August 1st		Visited M.V.S. + No. 4 Coy A.S.C. * revised esty attendance of units routine office work.	
"	2nd		Inspected animals 11th Cheshires + 5th Bedfords Regt. at N° 4 Coy A.S.C. + B.H.Q. 4112 Fld Amb.	
"	3rd		Visited O/C 50th M.V.S. Called at N° 4 Coy A.S.C. general routine office work.	
"	4th		Inspected 35 horses at N° 4 Coy A.S.C. prior to be transferred to Remounts routine office work.	
"	5th		Inspected animals of 116th Fld A.Q. 4185 "N" Fuslrs general routine office work.	
"	6th		Inspected 23 horses at N° 4 Coy A.S.C. for transfer to Remts. visited A.D.V.S. office visited M.V.S.	
"	7th		Visited 50th M.V.S. with A.D.V.S. Corps. inspected animals of "F" M.G. Bn., 1st Suffolks, 4th H.L.I. 11th Roy Scots.	
"	8th		Met A.D.V.S. Corps + inspected animals of 325 C.O.R.E. visited B.H.Q. general routine office work.	
"	9th		Inspected animals of 116th Bde H.Q. 18th "N" Fuslrs., 23rd "N" F's + 25th N.F. routine office work.	
"	10th		Inspected animals of B.H.Q. Inspected wallets of M.C. Sergts of 114th + 118th Inf Bdes., R.O.W.	
"	11th		Visited 50th M.V.S. arranged w 2 men to go to N° 19 V. Hosp. arranged with B.H.Q. re musketry course for M.V.S.	
"	12th		Inspected animals of Royal Scots, Suffolks, visited M.V.S. general routine office work.	
"	13th		Inspected animals of "E" M.G. Bn., visited 116th R.S.H.Q. visited B.H.Q. routine office work.	
"	14th		Visited M.V.S. delayed Capt Shelton's exam to Hosp, pending return of Capt Broadhurst A.V.C. visited A.D.V.S. Corps. Called at B.H.Q. re arrangements re moving, routine office work.	
"	15th		Travelled by car from Nielles-lez-Andres to Pouvrelez Mt Dieppe reported to D.D.V.S. & Offr. a then came on to Varengeville sur Mer.	

WAR DIARY

or

INTELLIGENCE SUMMARY.

(Erase heading not required.)

Army Form C. 2118.

Instructions regarding War Diaries and Intelligence Summaries are contained in F.S. Regs., Part II. and the Staff Manual respectively. Title pages will be prepared in manuscript.

Place	Date August 1918	Hour	Summary of Events and Information	Remarks and references to Appendices
Vavengeville Sur Mer.	16½		Office moved with D.H.Q. from Mollier les Andres arrived today at Vavengeville S. mer.	
"	17½		Inspected stabling of horses. No arrangements for office yet made.	
"	18½		Reported arrival in writing to D.D.V.S. L.of C. Inspected stabling &c.	
"	19½		General routine office work.	
"	20½		Called on D.D.V.S. L.of C. Had long interview with him. Office located in school.	
"	21st		Met D.D.V.S. L.of C. visited No 9 V.H. Vety Hospital. general routine office work.	
"	22nd		Inspected stabling of animals of D.H.Q. general routine office work.	
"	23rd		Inspected animals of No.225 Coy R.E. general routine office work.	
"	24½		General routine office work.	
"	25½		Inspected animals of 39th D.H.Q. stabling &c. routine office work.	
"	26½		General routine office work.	
"	27½		General routine office work.	
"	28½		Inspected D.H.Q. animals general routine office work.	
"	29½		Inspected animals of No.225 Coy R.E. routine office work.	
"	30½		General routine office work. weekly & monthly returns &c.	
"	31st		Called on D.V.S. L. of C. general routine office work.	

This formation was mobilised August 1915.
Arrived in France 6/3/1916

Harry Gull
Major
D.A.D.V.S.
O in charge

WAR DIARY or INTELLIGENCE SUMMARY

Army Form C. 2118.

Stout Confidential
B.M. D.V.S. 39th Division

98 31

Place	Date September 1918	Hour	Summary of Events and Information	Remarks and references to Appendices
Varengeville-S-Mer	1st		General routine office work.	
"	2nd		Gave lecture on general horse management & feeding.	
"	3rd		Inspected animals of D.H.Q., Runners &c. general office work.	
"	4th		Visited D.D.V.S. (Southern) re general work &c. routine office work.	
"	5th		Lecture of horse management, inspected grooming kit &c.	
"	6th		Completion of weekly returns, inspected horses of 225th Coy R.E. Headqrs.	
"	7th		Inspected animals of 116th Infantry Bde. HQ. Cadre Bns.	
"	8th		General routine office work.	
"	9th		Inspected animals of Divn Headquarters general routine office work	
"	10th		Visited D.D.V.S. (Southern) General routine office work.	
"	11th		Inspected animals of 118th Infantry Brigade routine office work.	
"	12th		Gave Lecture on Horse management &c. general routine office work.	
"	13th		General routine office work, completion of weekly returns.	
"	14th		Inspected animals HQ. 225th Coy R.E. routine office work.	
"	15th		General routine office work.	
"	16th		Gave Lectures on general horse management to D.H.Q. personnel	

Army Form C. 2118.

WAR DIARY
or
INTELLIGENCE SUMMARY.
(Erase heading not required.)

Instructions regarding War Diaries and Intelligence Summaries are contained in F. S. Regs., Part II. and the Staff Manual respectively. Title pages will be prepared in manuscript.

Place	Date	Hour	Summary of Events and Information	Remarks and references to Appendices
Vanengeold	September 1918			
Sun-Mon	17th		Visited office of D.D.V.S. (Southern) General routine office work.	
"	18th		Inspected animals of Div Headqrs. routine office work.	
"	19th		Gave lecture on general horse management to 225th Co personnel	
"	20th		Completion of weekly returns; general routine office work	
"	21st		Inspected animals of 117th Inf Bde general routine office work	
"	22nd		General routine office work.	
"	23rd		Gave lecture on general horse management to Div Headqrs personnel	
"	24th		Inspected animals of 225th Field Coy R.E. routine office work	
"	25th		Inspected animals of 118th Inf Brigade. routine office work.	
"	26th		Visited office D.D.V.S. (Southern) General routine office work.	
"	27th		Compilation of weekly returns. general routine office work.	
"	28th		Gave lecture on horse management to H.Q. 225th Co personnel	
"	29th		General routine office work.	
"	30.		Visited D.D.V.S. Office re general work. routine office work.	

This formation was mobilized Aug 1915.
— " — arrived in France 6/3/1916.

Harshee Major
D.A.D.V.S 39th Division

WAR DIARY or INTELLIGENCE SUMMARY

Army Form C. 2118.

D.A.D.V.S. 39th Division

No. L 33

Place	Date 1918	Hour	Summary of Events and Information	Remarks and references to Appendices
Vaumgrielle	October 1st		Inspected horses of 117th Bde. Headqrs. + cadre Battalions	
,,	2nd		Gave lecture on feeding of animals &c to 225th Coy. personnel	
,,	3rd		Inspected animals of 225th Coy. R.E. + grooming kit &c.	
,,	4th		Compilation of weekly returns, general routine office work.	
,,	5th		Inspected animals of 118th Inf. Bde + cadre Battalions	
,,	6th		General routine office work.	
,,	7th		Lecture on animal management, feeding &c. B.H.Q. personnel	
,,	8th		Visited D.D.V.S. (Southern) re general work, routine office work	
,,	9th		Inspected animals of B.H.Q. stables +grooming kit &c.	
,,	10th		Inspected animals of Headqrs. 225th Coy R.E., stables &c. routine office work.	
,,	11th		Compilation of weekly returns, general routine office work.	
,,	12th		Inspected animals of 116th Cadre Bttns. + Bde. H.Q.	
,,	13th		Inspected animals of 4th Bttn East Lancs Regt + 4/5 Bttn Sherwood Foresters	
,,	14th		General routine office work.	
,,	15th		Gave lecture on points of horses &c. B.H.Q. personnel	
,,	16th		Gave lecture on horse management, feeding &c. 225th Coy R.E. personnel	

Army Form C. 2118.

WAR DIARY
or
INTELLIGENCE SUMMARY.
(Erase heading not required.)

Instructions regarding War Diaries and Intelligence Summaries are contained in F. S. Regs., Part II. and the Staff Manual respectively. Title pages will be prepared in manuscript.

Place	Date 1918	Hour	Summary of Events and Information	Remarks and references to Appendices
Warenquiers	October			
Sun-men.	17th		Visited B.H.Qrs. (Southern) re general work &c. routine office work.	
"	18th		Completion of weekly returns, routine office work.	
"	19th		Inspected animals of 118th Inf. Bde H.Q. + Cadre Bttn.	
"	20th		General routine office work.	
"	21st		Lecture on horses - grooming, feeding &c. S.H.Q. personnel	
"	22nd		Inspected animals of 119th Bde Headqrs. + Cadre Bttns.	
"	23rd		Inspected animals of 13th also stables, grooming kit &c.	
"	24th		Inspected animals of H.Q. 225th Co. R.E. + gave lecture on grooming &c.	
"	25th		Completion of weekly returns, general routine office work.	
"	26th		Visited B.H.Qrs. (Southern) general routine office work.	
"	27th		General routine office work.	
"	28th		Inspected animals of 118th Inf. Bde H.Q. Cadre Bttn.	
"	29th		Inspected animals of 4th Bttn East Lancs + 4/5th Sherwood Fors.	
"	30th		Inspected animals of B.H.Q. stables, grooming kit &c.	
"	31st		Inspected animals of 228 Co R.E. stables grooming kit &c.	

This formation mobilized August 1915. Arrived in France, March 4th 1916. Maybee Major S/3/9/1915 39 CCW

14

Army Form C. 2118.

WAR DIARY
or
INTELLIGENCE SUMMARY.

(Erase heading not required.)

DA SVS. 39 Div.

Vol 3

Place	Date	Hour	Summary of Events and Information	Remarks and references to Appendices
November 1918. Varengeville Sur-Mer	1st		Inspected animals D.H.Q. M.M.P. general routine office work.	
"	2nd		General routine office work.	
"	3rd		Inspected animals of 225th Coy R.E. grooming hit 9a	
"	4th		Visited SVO's. Left to general routine office work.	
"	5th		Inspected stables of 39th M.M.P. grooming hit 9a	
"	6th		General routine office work.	
"	7th		Inspected stables &c of SVO. general routine office work.	
"	8th		Compilation of weekly returns. general routine office work.	
"	9th		Inspected stables &c of section of 225th Coy R.E.	
"	10th		General routine office work.	
"	11th		Proceeded on 14 days leave of absence to United Kingdom	
"	26th		Returned off leave.	
"	27th		Inspected horses stables D.H.Q. general routine office work	
"	28th		Inspected animals of 225th Coy R.E. general routine office work.	
"	29th		Had interviews with SVO's. LofC Southern. routine office work	
"	30th		Inspected horses of No 2 LofC Area Reception Camp routine office work.	

This formation mobilized August 1915. Left 1915 mob 4th 1918. Arrived in France march 4th 1918.

Harry Rees major
DA SVS 39 Div

2353 Wt W2514/7454 700,000 5/15 D.D. & L. A.D.S.S./Forms/2118.

WAR DIARY
or
INTELLIGENCE SUMMARY.
(Erase heading not required.)

Army Form C. 2118.

D.A.D.V.S. 39th Division

Place	Date 1918.	Hour	Summary of Events and Information	Remarks and references to Appendices
Vanenghem sur Mer	1st		Inspected animals of R.H.Q. & stables &c. routine office work.	
"	2nd		General routine office work.	
"	3rd		Visited D.D.V.S. L. of C. re general work routine office work.	
"	4th		Inspected animals of 119/15 Inf. Bde. general routine office work.	
"	5th		Inspected animals of M.M.P. stables kit &c. routine office work.	
"	6th		Compilation of weekly returns, general routine office work.	
"	7th		Inspected animals of H.80 & 604 A.S.C. general routine office work.	
"	8th		General routine office work.	
"	9th		Inspected animals of R.H.Q. stables &c. routine office work.	
"	10th		Had interview with D.D.V.S. L. of C. routine office work.	
"	11th		Inspected animals of 119/15 Inf. Bde. general routine office work.	
"	12th		Compilation of weekly returns. general routine office work.	
"	13th		General routine office work.	
"	14th		Inspected animals of M.M.P. & Stables grooming kit &c.	
"	15th		General routine office work.	
"	16th		Visited D.D.V.S. L. of C. general routine office work.	

Army Form C. 2118.

WAR DIARY
or
INTELLIGENCE SUMMARY.
(Erase heading not required.)

Instructions regarding War Diaries and Intelligence Summaries are contained in F. S. Regs., Part II. and the Staff Manual respectively. Title pages will be prepared in manuscript.

Place	Date	Hour	Summary of Events and Information	Remarks and references to Appendices
Vacquerie	December 1918			
	17th Mon		Inspected animals of BHQ - grooming kit - stables &c.	
"	18th		Inspected animals of 480th Coy R.A.S.C. routine office work.	
"	19th		General routine office work.	
"	20th		Compilation of weekly returns general routine office work.	
"	21st		Inspected stables grooming kit M.M.P. routine office work.	
"	22nd		General routine office work.	
"	23rd		Inspected animals of 119th Inf Bde routine office work.	
"	24th		Inspected animals of 116th Inf Bde "	
"	25th		General routine office work.	
"	26th		Inspected animals BHQ and stables &c routine office work.	
"	27th		Compilation of weekly returns general routine office work.	
"	28th		Inspected animals of 480th Coy A.S.C. routine office work.	
"	29th		Inspected animals of M.M.P. & stables &c routine office work.	
"	30th		Classifying animals for demobilization.	Hereby 30 months
"	31st		Classifying animals for demobilization.	
			This formation mobilized August 1915. arrived in France Mch 4th 1916.	

WAR DIARY
or
INTELLIGENCE SUMMARY.
(Erase heading not required.)

Army Form C. 2118

Instructions regarding War Diaries and Intelligence Summaries are contained in F.S. Regs., Part II. and the Staff Manual respectively. Title pages will be prepared in manuscript.

Place	Date	Hour	Summary of Events and Information	Remarks and references to Appendices
Tonquières sur mer	January 1919			
	1st		Inspected animals RHQ M.M.P. grooming kit. stables &c.	
"	2nd		General routine office work.	
"	3rd		Visited D.D.V.S. L.of.C. re embarkation of horses from Dieppe routine office work.	
"	4th		Inspected HQ animals general routine office work	
"	5th		General routine office work	
"	6th		Animals of No 3 B.R.B. classified for demob. by Vety Board	
"	7th		Inspected animals of 119th Infy Bde. routine office work.	
"	8th		Inspected animals of 480th Coy RASC general routine work	
"	9th		General routine office work. Visited D.D.V.S. L.of.C.	
"	10th		Animals of Cavalry Corps School classified for demobilization	
"	11th		Visited D.D.V.S. L.of.C. re classification of horses for demobilization	
"	12th		General routine office work.	
"	13th		Animals of 39th Divl. Headqrs & 260th Coy RASC classified for demob.	
"	14th		Visited M.L.O. Dieppe re embarkation of animals	
"	15th		Inspected 302 animals at Dieppe prior to embarkation	
"	16th		General routine office work.	

Army Form C. 2118.

WAR DIARY
or
INTELLIGENCE SUMMARY.
(Erase heading not required.)

Instructions regarding War Diaries and Intelligence Summaries are contained in F. S. Regs., Part II and the Staff Manual respectively. Title pages will be prepared in manuscript.

D.A.D.V.S. 39th Divn

Place	Date	Hour	Summary of Events and Information	Remarks and references to Appendices
Kavengalla	January 1919			
Sun. men.	17	8	Compilation of weekly returns, general routine office work.	
"	18	15	Animals of A.A.O Depot & Regtl. 280ᵗʰ Coy R.A.S.C. classified	
"	19	15	Animals of Transport Le Treport & 7 I.R Depot Men's classified.	
"	20	15	Animals of 224ᵗʰ Coy R.A.S.C. & P.O. Wideamps classified.	
"	21	30	Animals of 2/6ᵗʰ Bn L.b. Inf & 15ᵗʰ Bn Essex Regt classified	
"	22	30	Animals of 501ˢᵗ Coy R.A.S.C. & animals of St Saens area classified	
"	23	30	Visited D.D.V.S. L.ofC. general routine office work.	
"	24	8	Compilation of weekly returns routine office work.	
"	25	30	Animals of 147ᵗʰ Inf Bde Y.M.P. at St Saens & Dieppe classified.	
"	26	15	Animals of N⁰ 2 Reinforcement Camp classified.	
"	27	15	General routine office work.	
"	28	15	Evacuated 5 animals from B.H.Q. to N⁰ 9 Vety Hospital.	
"	29	8	Compilation of return of all animals classified from 6/11/19 to 29/1/19.	
"	30	15	Visited D.D.V.S. L.ofC. general routine office work.	
"	31		Compilation of weekly returns.	

This formation mobilized August 1915. arrived in France 4ᵗʰ Mch. 1916.

Harry Beale Major
D.A.D.V.S. 39th Divn